LIFE IS GRAND
AFTER THAT MAN

RELATIONSHIP RECOVERY
TECHNIQUES FOR WOMEN

LIFE IS GRAND
AFTER THAT MAN

RELATIONSHIP RECOVERY
TECHNIQUES FOR WOMEN

DR. SHANTEL THOMAS

Contents

Part Three
Life Is Grand Again: Preparing For The Next Relationship

This book is dedicated to the many women who have walked through the doors of A Sound Mind Counseling Service after having been hurt by an unhealthy relationship. For every woman who shared a story of pain, grief, worthlessness, or damaged self-esteem, I thank you. I dedicate this book to you because you survived THAT MAN. Now your tenacity, triumph and inspiration will be shared with other women. Continue to persevere.

Acknowledgments

To my sons, Gideon and Micah. You have been the biggest blessings of my life; you are my everything. Though you are young, I am constantly in awe of your intelligence, wit and creativity. I thank you both for your encouragement and ability to help me remain focused on this project. I am very honored and proud that God chose me as your mother.

A special thank you goes out to my mother, who is my biggest fan and enthusiast. Mom, I can always count on you. You have, and always will be, the wind beneath my wings. You are the very reason I am who I am today. If it were not for you telling me, "Shanny, you can do anything you put your mind to," I probably would not have accomplished half of the things I have in my life. I love you very much. Thank you for those words that continue to push me, even today.

To my father, Willie Brown, thank you for being the example of a true man. You showed me how a man is to treat a woman, told me things to make me wiser and more responsible, and educated me on the ways of life and men. I love for your patience and understanding when it came to raising a strong-willed young lady like me.

To my extended family, thank you for making me laugh my way through the difficult times and being supportive all the time. To my girlfriends, thank you just for being you. I love and need you all in my life.

Finally, I thank all the women who were a part of this project. Your stories truly inspired me, and your suggestion that I put my ideas into a book encouraged me to continue when life got in the way. Thank you for sharing your pain, sadness and heart wounds. I thank you all for allowing me to be a part of your relationship recovery process and for allowing me to use your stories to help other women who are on the same journey. Without you, this book would not have come to fruition.

Introduction

When I started my private practice in 1999 I had a number of women, from the very young to the very old, come to counseling due to a relationship breakup. While these women came from different backgrounds, professions, and so on, they all shared something in common: each felt betrayed by the man she had been dating. Over years of treating these women I found there were repetitive "types of men." One day after a session a client said to me, "Dr. Thomas, I have been to other therapists but they never broke down my emotions, the type of man that I have been choosing, or the ways to recover the way you have for me. I think you should write a book about it. I would buy it and I know it will help a lot of women."

I wrote this book to look at dysfunctional relationships. Many women, myself included, tend to be fixers of people, situations and things. While we are trying to fix things, however, we often end up being hurt in relationships, especially intimate relationships. Everyone grows up in a home with some dysfunction on some level. For some women, seeing their mothers (and sometimes their fathers) stay in dysfunctional relationships created a breeding ground for the same behaviors to develop.

Throughout this book I use the term "THAT MAN" to refer to men who lie, cheat, beat or otherwise mistreat women. These men are dysfunctional, and they rarely take into consideration the wants and needs of their partners. When a woman deals with "THAT MAN," she is left damaged and wounded. He preys on her desires to be in a relationship and exploits her intelligence and her abilities along the way. THAT MAN drains the woman emotionally, financially, spiritually and even sexually. The good news is, there are ways to recover from THAT MAN. The women I have counseled over the years are proof of this, and they have helped me develop a set of activities and techniques to set yourself free from pain and move on to a happier life.

In the pages that follow, I will share with you the process of healing. The first section will help you identify the type of dysfunctional man you have dealt with in the past. The second section talks about the ways you can reclaim your mind, body and spirit after you have left THAT MAN, and the last section helps you move forward and begin healing. It also focuses on preparing for your next relationship. It is my sincere hope that these tools will support and assist you in letting go of the past and rediscovering the strength and beauty that has been inside you all along.

Part One
THAT MAN Brought Me Pain

Financial Fabio (The Greedy Man)

"I came home and he had taken everything! He told me that he wouldn't do that! We had agreed that when he moved out I would give him money and he would leave me all of the furniture and household items. He lied to me again. He took everything!"

I have heard this story too many times. Man lies to woman over and over; woman trusts man to keep his word and do right by her, only to be disappointed or devastated once again. You're angry with him, and even angrier with yourself for being tricked into believing his lies. You ask yourself, "Why this keeps happening?" Well, just like a man, you can be impressed by good looks. You see him? He has tight abs, strong biceps, a gorgeous smile and an enticing masculine scent.

When a woman goes for a man with good looks and trusts his lies, her mind shuts down and she begins to think with her heart and not her head. Sound familiar? If so, this was the beginning of the problem for you.

How many times has a friend begun a relationship with a guy you know is wrong for her? You try to educate, talk to or just inform your friend of the ways of the guy, only to hear, "That isn't true. He's not like that" But

1

every time they go out, she is paying for everything: dinner, movies, drinks, concerts, trips, and so on.

Or, maybe you are this woman, and you have refused to heed the warnings of friends who tell you to get away from Financial Fabio.

Financial Fabio is skilled at hoodwinking and bamboozling the women he dates. He tells you how attractive your financial independence is to him, saying things like, "I love that you can pay, that turns me on." According to the Bible, men are supposed to be the providers, protectors and priests over their home, yet Financial Fabio is very good at tricking you into becoming the man in your relationship.

A few years ago I worked with a woman who made over a half-million dollars a year. She had a beautiful home in an exclusive neighborhood and she drove a shiny, high-end vehicle. On numerous occasions she came into my office and told me about her boyfriend, who continually borrowed large sums of money from her. He always had a sad story about his mother or some other family member who was in need of his help.

In the beginning of the relationship he paid her back; by six months in, however, he had stopped giving her a cent. At this point he owed her well over $15,000, and he would yell at her, call her names and start fights with her whenever she mentioned the subject of repayment. He would then leave the home, only to return several days later acting as if nothing had happened.

Fast-talking and suave, Financial Fabios continually manipulate you out of your money. Over the years I have talked with women who have encountered two different types of Fabios: Jacks and Gigolos.

The Jacks have great ideas, business plans or sad family stories that they use to get your money quickly. Jacks have a little bit of money so they appear capable of financing dates and the relationship. Over time, you find out that your Jack's resources are very limited, but by then it is usually too late. You are already in love with him and do not believe you can find anyone else with more charisma.

The Gigolos, on the other hand, are the guys who continually sweet talk women out of their belongings. They say all the romantic words that make you feel good but they can never give you the financial backing you need to sustain the household.

Jacks and Gigolos are the reason a lot of women find themselves in "financial follies." This happens when you know you should not continue to finance the relationship but you do so thinking you will eventually get an engagement ring as a reward.

I have counseled numerous women who said, "After all I have done for him financially, I know the ring is on the way. Shoot, I'm the one who paid for him to get through college so I know he is going to marry me!"

Not necessarily. Paying for college, buying a car or a house does not mean he is now obligated to marry you. Many women told me they thought THAT MAN would realize he could depend on her, feel secure enough with her money-saving behaviors, and ultimately propose to her.

You have to remember that the job of Jacks and Gigolos is to make you feel good about yourself and your financial responsibility. Then they take advantage of it. These men praise you and make you feel very intelligent and powerful. That is the key to their ability to manipulate you. If a Jack or Gigolo connects to your mental and financial self, then he's maneuvered you right where he wants you. A Jack is attracted to your intellect, so the relationship may involve minimal sexual intercourse. He likes you, but not *that* much. He may even be pretending to care about you. A Gigolo, on the other hand, knows his way around the bedroom. He is very promiscuous and has many women he is entertaining on a regular basis.

Another example: I once knew a man who said, "I don't ever need to touch a woman physically (meaning sexually) to get her wrapped around my fingers. All I need to do is make love to her mind and I can have whatever I want from her." This man knows that women really enjoy being romanced and spoken to about their success. He had learned how to get into a woman's head and heart by telling her what she needed to hear and showing her worth.

We *do* love to receive flowers, candy, cards and gifts. And when a man sends flowers to the office, we really love it, because then our coworkers see how much he cares. In some cases this might be true, but when you're dealing with THAT MAN it's just a form of manipulation, and you're all caught up in it. With this simple gesture of affection, he has made you believe he really loves you. He has found another way to get into your heart without ever connecting to you on a physical level, and he is ready to present his case for another cash advance.

Another example: Let's say you come home from work and he has run a warm bath for you. You can smell the lavender in the air. He takes off your clothes piece by piece, picks you up then sits you down in the tub. He bathes you, massages your body and dries you off with a warm towel. Your man lotions your body down with your favorite scented lotion, dresses you in your favorite relaxing outfit, and tells you to relax while he makes your dinner. When the meal is ready, he feeds you every bite, then you cuddle up to watch a movie and fall asleep in his arms.

You awaken the next day only to find he went home while you slept. He never tried to make love to you. He only served you and left you feeling completely satisfied. Then three days later he comes to you with some story about needing to borrow $500 to pay some bills. You reminisce on the wonderful experiences you had with THAT MAN and do not hesitate to give him the cash. You have just been taken by a Jack.

When you are dating a man who is constantly broke, something is terribly wrong. If he frequently complains that his ex-girlfriend is taking all of his money for child support or the divorce caused him to be financially unstable, the question you should ask is, Should I be dating this man at all? The answer may not always be black and white, but there is one thing I do know: women need to go back to some of the old dating rules. They were put in place for a reason. You have to learn to let a man be a man.

For example, if a gentleman asks you out, isn't he supposed to pay for the date? Yes! Traditionally, I was told a man should pay for the first five dates before he asks a woman to go Dutch or pay for the date completely. Certainly, you should not *offer* to pay for a date until you have gone out with him at least five times.

One reason for the dinner rule is to allow you to see if the man is financially stable. Today women are quick to show that they are financially capable and independent, which can cause them to miss out on some valuable information. Don't misunderstand me; I am all for women displaying their financial independence; they just need to learn to exhibit it at the right time.

After hearing stories like these for years from my female clientele, I have come up with a list of questions all women should ask themselves in order to avoid Financial Fabio in the future:

1. Does he live alone?

A man cannot be a man if he is still living in his mother's, sister's, friend's house or basement, for free. A man must be able to provide for a woman. He should have a steady income that he brings into the home on a regular basis. Please stop falling for the, "I moved in to help her out" line too. No grown man moves in with his able-bodied, sixty-five-year-old working mother to help her out (and he doesn't have a job).

Also, stop falling for the "My friend almost lost his home so I moved in to help him pay the mortgage." If he is paying his friend $200 a month, I doubt that is really helping out much. Think about it. Where else could THAT MAN go and live for $200 a month?

2. Does he have a car of his own?

If so, does he pay for it in full by himself every month, or is he getting help from family or friends? If he is not able to pay all of his bills by himself, ask yourself, "What will he be able to do for me?"

Hopefully, you come to the conclusion that the answer is, "Nothing right now."

If he is continually asking you for $20 or borrowing $50 from his sister to maintain his monthly bills, he is not good with his money. The Bible says, "A good man leaves an inheritance for his children's children" (Proverbs13:22). He can't leave an inheritance for his children if he cannot manage his money.

If he cannot meet his basic needs (food, clothing, shelter) on his own, then how do you expect him to help you meet yours? A wise woman does not continue to remain with a man who has been evicted three or four times in one year. This signals a repeat pattern of financial instability. Don't allow THAT MANto make your house his next stop.

3. *Does he have a savings and a checking account?*

Do not let him tell you he does not like banks, so he keeps all his money on him. The truth of the matter could be that he has bounced so many checks no bank will allow him to have an account until he pays off the overdraft fees. If he cannot show you his bank account it's probably because he doesn't have one. The other possibility is that he may not know how to open an account or balance a checkbook.

4. *Ask to see his credit report*

I know for some of you this is a scary thing. But if he cares for you he will have no problem showing it to you. We all have had some bad credit days, but he should be willing to show and share these issues with you. His score may not be perfect, but at least you know what you are dealing with and he can explain all of his past financial errors.

5. *Does he use payday loans?*

Payday loans are the twenty-first-century version of a loan shark; they charge very high interest fees that cut deeply into your income. If your man is constantly telling you that he took out such a loan or if he uses payday loans to live from one week to the next, he is probably going to need your help financially.

6. Does he have a credit card?

If he does, does he use it wisely? A person should not use their credit cards to purchase food or small amounts of gasoline, or pay small bills. If your guy is demonstrating this behavior, know he is bound to ask you for some financial assistance. If he cannot get a credit card on his own, please do not help him.

I am not saying that every man who has one or two financial issues is bad. But a man who lives by using one of the six scenarios listed above on a regular basis is a Financial Fabio and will at some point try to take you.

Abusive Adam
(The Mentally and Physically Abusive Man)

"Shan, come get me! He just hit me again. I think he broke my nose! Please come get me. I'm at the White Castle down the street. I just need someone to go to the hospital with me. I'm afraid to go alone."

While in college I had a girlfriend who was in a physically abusive relationship. I remember being in class the day she called me crying and yelling into the phone. The abuse had occurred before; in fact, it had been happening for two years. This time he blackened her eye, and she finally said, "Enough is enough!" When you are dealing with a man who is physically abusive, sometimes it takes a while for you to see your way out.

Abusive Adams do a wonderful job of making you feel insecure, afraid, doubtful and confused. You must understand that the goal of this type of man is to degrade and belittle you in order to keep you in the relationship. Abusive Adams build and maintains their power and control by telling you lies about their abilities and intelligence. This is the way they penetrate your mind and spirit. To recover from the mental, spiritual and physical attacks of Abusive Adams and get your life back on track, you must reconnect with your true self and regain your power and control of your mind. You must also create an escape plan. This takes strength, courage and wisdom.

A man who hits a woman has his own personal issues that he needs to overcome. He is like a Dr. Jekyll/Mr. Hyde, so beware of him if he tries to come around again.

Remember the story? Dr. Jekyll was an intelligent, mild-mannered man, but physically he was very weak. He had a hard time communicating with others and had a difficult time with women. To overcome his feelings of powerlessness, he created an alter ego named Mr. Hyde, who he intended to be suave and debonair. Instead, all of the ugly tendencies deep inside of Dr. Jekyll came out. Mr. Hyde stalked women and ran through the community, wreaking destruction on everything and everyone. He also killed women nightly for fun.

The same is true of Abusive Adams. This kind of man hits women and degrades them because he truly feels that way himself. Abusive Adam makes you afraid of everything. He also isolates you from everyone, sometimes for so long that you may forget how to connect with your family and girlfriends. You may even be afraid to socialize and make new friends.

His goal is to make you afraid to think, move, or act. THAT MAN wants you to be totally dependent on him in every way, so he makes you feel you cannot make a decision on your own. Another way he dominates you is to make you believe you can't do anything right — be it cooking, cleaning, caring for the kids or even being able to pick your own clothes or hairstyle. THAT MAN's ultimate goal is to destroy your very existence by devastating your sense of self-worth and causing mental confusion.

Before you were involved with Abusive Adam you were confident about your abilities. After dealing with Abusive Adam, you don't trust yourself to do anything without him. THAT MAN has stolen your joy.

Recognize Abusive Adam when you see him. Some Adams are around for a long time and some for a brief moment. If a man hits you once, there is a high probability that he will strike you again. Please understand that in some abusive relationships, the physical abuse is the last thing to surface. Sometimes you go through months, even years of emotional, verbal and mental abuse before the violence starts. In other situations, it happens right from the beginning.

Some women are unclear about the different types of abuse. They are physical, mental, emotional, sexual and verbal. A man who hits, kicks, punches or spits on you is being physically abusive. A man who tells you that he is coming over but never comes or comes two hours late is being mentally abusive. A man who gets upset with you and withholds his affection from you is being emotionally abusive. A sexually abusive man forces you to have sex with him when you are sick or tired. Or he may take sex from you when you are sleeping. Finally, a man is verbally abusive to you when he continually calls you out of your name or puts you down.

When abuse has gone on for some time, you may begin to minimize or even deny that it is abuse. I have had women say to me in therapy, "It's not that bad." Or, "I have experienced worse with other guys." Or, "I caused him to behave that way…it is all my fault."

At times, denial may be the only thing you can do to stop from losing your mind. Whatever you do to survive the abuse is to be commended. You have survived. You are still alive. Now it is time for you to redefine yourself after leaving THAT MAN.

Being abused is a devastating experience, and the wounds may take years to heal. But be comforted, because you are now on your way out, or possibly you are already out completely. He may have been a master of deceit and fear, but you were the victor because you walked away from that horror. Some women are embarrassed to speak of the abuse, but there is much power in telling your story to someone else.

The fastest way for a woman to heal is through talking. The more you talk, the more you release the pain and the better you feel. Some women are private or embarrassed of the abuse, or don't want to seem too chatty; however, if there is any time it's beneficial to speak out, it's now, so do it. Your words are powerful; they empower you, cleanse your soul and heal you and others along the way. As you speak you begin to hear your own voice…your own story. You then process your past behaviors better and begin to recognize more clearly the work you need to do so you never go down that path again.

I know you do not want to recall this part of your life. But the fact you may have had black eyes, broken bones, or been tied down and whipped are part of you is critical to your recovery process. In fact, the strength that you had to keep your sanity and not lose your mind through all the beatings, name-calling and embarrassing moments in public is enough for you to truly congratulate yourself, buy yourself a rose or take a relaxing trip for a few days.

First and foremost, remember that you have a sound mind; you are a beautiful and phenomenal woman. Go back in your mind to who you were before you met THAT MAN. What were your dreams, passions goals and desires?

Did you see yourself in college? Owning your own business? Inventing something? Whatever it was, you need to begin to refocus your mind and spirit on it again.

Do not allow the negative thoughts behaviors and actions of THAT MAN to destroy your inner voice and spirit that told you, "You can do whatever you put your mind to!" My friend, it is okay to begin again and live your life to the fullest! Celebrate, because life is grand AFTER THAT MAN!

Begin Again

Granted, he was a hateful, mean, abusive male, but he is the last you will ever be with. The words you begin to speak over yourself will decide your path from this day forward.

As women, we need to affirm ourselves. Start by creating a list of ten things you can say to yourself about you. For example, "I am beautiful and worthy to be treated with love and respect."

It may feel false at first, but as you continue to speak these affirmations over yourself, you will begin to believe them. This is the power of positive speaking in action. The more you speak about who you are the better you will feel, because you manifest whatever you put into the atmosphere. This is what therapists call positive "self-talk."

THAT MAN tried to destroy the essence of who you were but he couldn't do it. Now take back your authority: Open your mouth and speak about the awesome, powerful woman that you are.

Again, our words have power. If you become afraid to speak out about your abuse you lose your way and you lose your power. Your power lies in your voice. So begin to use your voice now. It will help you to tell your story, and every chapter of that story was necessary for you to become the woman you are today. Your story will help your children, friends and even people you don't know. Once you speak life over yourself and begin to share your story, others will begin to be healed and gain personal power to leave THAT MAN, as you did. Remember, your past is behind you but your future lies ahead.

So how will your story begin? What will the middle chapters include? What will you leave for your children to share? Do not be ashamed about the chapters that include your pain. Everyone's life has some chapters of pain. If not, we would not have truly lived. You would not have learned to be resilient if you had never experienced any hardships or challenges.

To avoid the next Abusive Adam, ask yourself:

1. Does he want to know where you are at every moment?

These types of men generally will call you all the time, wonder where you are and who you are with. I even know of some men who have said, "I'll buy her a cell phone and pay the bill, just so I can see who she was talking to."

Ladies, beware. I'm not saying that all men who want to pay your cell phone bill are abusive. What I am saying is that if his phone is locked, or he has a separate plan; won't let you see his phone; or has a second phone, you need to begin to question why he wants to get you a phone and pay your bill.

If he is always asking to see your phone and constantly asks, "What number is that?" or "Who are you talking to?" you have an Abusive Adam.

Other telltale signs include: driving by your house unannounced and saying he was "just in the neighborhood." That is one of Abusive Adam's favorite tricks. He may live and work on the other side of town, but he'll always find the time to pop up unannounced, thinking he will catch you doing something.

2. *Does he tell you what to wear when you go out?*

I once worked with a woman who told me her man always laid out her clothes before they went out. She said, "He is so nice and I love that about him." Once, when she decided she didn't want to wear what he put out for her, he began to curse at her, pushed her down onto the bed and told her that if she did not put on the outfit she would not be able to attend the dinner. She said she was afraid of him, because he had never acted in such a way. She then put on the outfit, but he still told her she could not attend the dinner. He then cut up the outfit and the other outfit she was going to wear.

This is Abusive Adam's way of intimidating his girlfriend. Remember, his goal is to create fear and damage her self-esteem. Even if he buys two new outfits to replace the ones he cut up, his objective of having the power in the relationship and controlling your every move has been achieved. A lot of you want to minimize this behavior and say, "Well, he apologized and bought me a new outfit too." The problem is, this kind of behavior not only continues but intensifies with each incident.

Stop minimizing and making excuses for THAT MAN's behavior. A real man would never buy all of your clothing, then tell you on what day and what time to wear it. A real man understands that the gift is YOU and the clothing just accentuates the package! Remember, you are the queen and must be treated with love and respect. As long as you remember this, Abusive Adam will not be able to break your spirit.

3. Does he call you names and put you down?

If he constantly tells you how unattractive you are, or you how you should feel lucky he wants you because no one else does, you are dealing with an Abusive Adam. A man who loves you would never put you down or degrade you. If every time you go out he is looking at another woman or telling you how you need to work out to look more like someone else, THAT MAN *is Abusive Adam.*

Maybe he says things like, "You know, you aren't all that cute but your body is banging and that is why I stay with you." Ladies, this is not a compliment. It is an insult. He just put you down. He will never affirm you for who you are, because he doesn't believe you deserve it.

Sometimes Abusive Adam is very subtle in his approach. He doesn't come out forcefully and loud but instead gets his degrading comments in through humor and sarcasm. Recognize that this is very damaging to your self-esteem. Do not be so desperate to have a man that you allow THAT MAN to talk to you any kind of way. You would be better off alone.

4. Does he spit on you, pinch you, or smack your butt so hard that it leaves a bruise every time? Does he then try to make light of it by saying, "Girl, I was just playing…"

This is abuse and, again, I want you to understand that with every incident the cycle intensifies. If you find yourself staying out late at the store or going over to a girlfriend's house to avoid going home due to fear, you are dealing with an Abusive Adam. If the thought of seeing him and leaving him both invoke fear in you, THAT MAN is an Abusive Adam, and I strongly encourage you to create an escape plan.

Ladies, there are many women's shelters and battered women's shelters ready to help you leave that abusive situation. You can locate the one in your area or call the National Domestic Violence Hotline at 800-799-SAFE for assistance in locating one.

5. Does he find fault with ALL of your friends?

If you are with an abusive male, none of your friends will be good enough for you to hang out with. I have heard things like: "I had to stop being friends with my best friend from kindergarten because she wasn't married," or "I had to give up my sorority activities because he said they were man-haters."

Wait just a moment. ALL the women in the sorority are man-haters? You give up your best friend for life because a man you met one year ago (or less) says so?

Maybe she tried to warn you about him or she started to see his abusive ways. Think hard about this. Best friends are hard to come by, especially ones you can truly trust and confide in, so don't let THAT MAN cause you to lose someone you have been able to count on all your life.

Do not allow THAT MAN to separate you from your family and friends. If you do, he will have you just where he wants you — all alone and totally dependent on him. He has all the power and control and you have lost everything.

You must stay connected to your support system at all costs, even if it means getting a separate cell phone. This is a lifeline and a critical tool in any escape plan. With your family to help, you can get out of that relationship before it leaves you with emotional and physical scars.

Bipolar Brad (The Emotionally Unstable Man)

"Dr. Thomas, this past week has been crazy! When I left home at eleven a.m. my husband was in the bed with the drapes closed, the lights turned out, curled up in a ball and crying his eyes out. When I came home at eight p.m. he was jumping up and down in the living room, he had ordered five large pizzas and soda, he was talking very fast and not making any sense. Then he stayed up for three days doing this same type of behavior. He was driving me and the kids crazy. He really scared me."

Many women at some point in their lives have had a mentally unstable boyfriend and just weren't aware of it. These are the type of men who say one thing but constantly do another. They make promises they never plan to keep. These broken promises leave you wounded and questioning your abilities, talents, intelligence and beauty. Relationships with these types of men cause you to doubt yourself and even cause you to think you are "crazy" at times.

These are the men who remind you of your father who was not around yet promised he would be there. A lot of us remember a time when our mother told us, *"Your father is on the way to get you"* and you sat by the door for hours and Daddy never showed up. You would ask your mom to fix your hair and put you in your favorite dress because you wanted to be Daddy's pretty little girl when he showed up.

Your father was supposed to arrive at 3 p.m. and you were excited. But 3:30 came and 4:30 p.m. came, and so on and your daddy never showed up. Finally, your mother came to the window you had been sitting at for hours, tapped you on the shoulder, and told you to go to bed because your daddy wasn't coming. You responded, "Mommy, he is coming. I know he is this time." Perhaps you even slept by the windowsill all night long waiting on him.

Little girls have high hopes that their dads will show up, and when they don't the daddy damage begins. The behavior, waiting for dad, hoping he would show, believing in him and going through this cycle over and over again sets the woman up for emotionally and mentally abusive relationships and she doesn't even know it. Like your dad, these men are inconsistent and inconsiderate, and while many men without mental illness act this way, the possibility is something you should be aware of. I call these men "Bipolar Brads."

Bipolar Brad often acts so erratically that you don't know whether you are coming or going. One minute he is yelling at you, calling you everything but a child of God, and the next he comes to you, tells you he loves you and wants to make love as if nothing happened. This is typical Bipolar Brad behavior. Bipolar Brad constantly does ridiculous things, but when you ask him about his behavior, he acts as if nothing is wrong. He may even ask why you are acting so "weird."

Bipolar Brad changes his mind about critical things in his life daily. You may come home from work one day to find that he has decided to quit his job. There was no discussion about it. He quit because he didn't like his boss. Bipolar Brad never thinks about how his actions affect other people. He did not consider that his not having an income will affect the entire household. He is only concerned with his needs being met and getting immediate gratification from everything he does.

Bipolar Brad has extreme moods swings. He is easily irritated, suffers from depression and has manic episodes. Bipolar disorder is a mental illness in which a person swings back and forth between deep depression and euphoria, or mania. Some people cycle very quickly between their moods, while others cycle very slowly. Their activity levels might be extremely high or low, and it may be hard for the person to carry out day-to-day tasks. People with bipolar disorder usually damage their relationships. They may have a record of poor job or school performance, go on sexual or substance abuse binges, get involved in other addictive behavior, and even attempt suicide.

A female in a relationship with Bipolar Brad may see him go from being very violent to very withdrawn to very happy and very sad, all in the same day. A Bipolar Brad may also have a very high sex drive for months on end while in a manic phase, but when depressed has little to no desire for physical intimacy. Either way, this can be very challenging for the woman he is in a relationship with.

Because his bipolar is going untreated, his mood swings become the focal point of the relationship and therefore the relationship is very unstable. Bipolar Brad's mood shifts so rapidly, the woman may begin to question her own state of mind; or, she may develop a nurturing spirit, caring for him as if he were her son. She will try to improve his state of mind by offering small things like running his bath water, making him dinner nightly, ironing his clothes and helping him with financial needs as well. She does these things not because she likes doing them, but to keep the peace in the home.

Other women may develop low self-esteem behind dealing with a Bipolar Brad. They may doubt their own intelligence due to what their Bipolar Brad says in his fits of rage or his very long depressive episodes.

Instead of going to therapy to work through these issues, Bipolar Brads will often project them onto the women they date and bring constant havoc into their world.

When you deal with this type of man, you may have constant thoughts and images of him

with other women, engaging in other negative activities, or even hurting himself or others. These images are another attack on your mind and your self-esteem.

Ultimately, these thoughts can become so overwhelming that you are uncertain about any of your decisions when it comes to the relationship. You begin to dislike all women because you are constantly comparing yourself in your mind to them. Bipolar Brad has made you believe that you doesn't measure up to other ladies.

Then when you see the former girlfriend out on the street and he introduces you to her, you look her up and down as if she has done something to you. She does not deserve to be accused or attacked by you. Also, you will look crazy for "mean mugging" her for no reason. Instead of going after her, remind yourself, that you are gorgeous and "ALL THAT."

Bipolar Brad is different from Abusive Adam in that Bipolar Brad has a mental disorder, meaning his behavior is based solely on the chemical imbalance in the brain which causes his mental state to become unstable. Whereas Abusive Adam wants to gain power and control over you, Bipolar Brad is struggling with his own state of mind and does not know how to manage his emotions. He can become a healthy, caring partner once he is on the proper medication and his mood is stabilized.

Here are some other mental illnesses that may impact the relationship. This is not a complete list and these are simple definitions of my own. Please consult with a mental health professional for a more in-depth understanding of any mental health issue.

Generalized Anxiety Disorder:

This disorder is characterized by a lot of different symptoms, two of which are excessive worry and excessive fear. A lot of us worry about family, friends and finances, but for someone with generalized anxiety disorder these worries run through the mind all day and night. They cause problems with sleeping, eating and may cause irritability. Some people develop irritable bowel, ulcers, and other physical conditions.

Narcissistic Personality Disorder:

A person with narcissistic personality disorder is extremely self-centered and always concerned with how they look, what they do, and how much power they have. A male with narcissistic personality disorder will be very vain and selfish, have feelings of entitlement, and always need to be the center of attention. He also usually lacks empathy for others and will always consider himself to be superior to them — including those in his inner circle of friends.

Antisocial Personality Disorder:

A person with antisocial personality disorder has no regard for authority, including the legal system. He has impulse control issues and exhibits a lot of aggressive behavior towards others. A male with antisocial personality disorder will have numerous run-ins with the law and constantly claims this is not his fault (i.e., that he was framed or accused of a crime that he did not commit).

These are just some of the more common disorders of adulthood. There are many others that can be researched on the Internet, or you can consult with a mental health professional if you believe your man is possibly a Bipolar Brad.

Let's go back to the story of the little girl. By the time she stops justifying and minimizing her father's behaviors and begins to accept him for who he is, the Daddy Damage has been done. Let's say the cycle of emotional abuse, broken promises, heartaches, hurt and deep pain started at age five and now she is sixteen years old — just in time for her to have her first boyfriend. This first boyfriend has the same characteristics as her dad, and she falls in love with him, thus the cycle of emotional abuse begins again. She wants him to love her and she will do anything so he doesn't leave her.

This little girl has learned from her father to accept excuses every time he did not show up. She believed him when he said things like, "My car broke down. I had to work late, or I fell asleep."

She learned to say, "It is okay, Daddy, I forgive you." But then he does it again and again. She has learned to continue trying because "nice girls" always give people another chance. Her father taught her this for eleven years, so how can she not give her boyfriend have the same number of chances when he says, "My car broke down. I had to work late, or I fell asleep." She has to be forgiving, nice and kind.

He may arrive two hours late, come in very happy and say something like, "Hey baby, sorry you had to wait but you know I had to take my time to look good for you (narcissism), or "I was so scared to get on the highway because of the bad storm that I had a panic attack in the house and couldn't drive over here" (panic disorder).

If you were that little girl, you might just greet him with a smile, while inside you are very angry. Why? Because he has already done this same thing on several other occasions.

He then sees that you will accept this type of behavior and believes it is okay with you if he's late every time. And you will continue to minimize his actions and keep thinking that being in this relationship is fine. You even justify behaviors, saying things like, "Oh, he is running a little late because it is storming out" or "Well, he does need to look good for me."

Just as with physical abuse, women who are emotionally abused may also minimize the behavior. Say, for instance, he doesn't return your call for an entire day, but the next day you call from a girlfriend's phone and he picks right up.

You say, "Hey, why didn't you call me?" And he says, "Oh my phone was dead," or "I left my phone in the car all night."

You then go from being angry at him to thinking, "Oh, I was going to break up with him, but he just forgot to charge his phone."

If this is a repeat behavior and he is always "forgetting" his phone or leaving it in the car overnight, you need to ask what's going on.

Don't accept any kind of man just to say you have one. Stop justifying his actions and realize you deserve better than what he is trying to give you — which is only half of himself. Again, some men are inconsistent, inconsiderate and unreliable because they are mentally ill; others are just badly behaved. You need to know the difference between the two.

Whatever the reason for Bipolar Brad's behavior, refuse to allow him to attack your character and make you feel that you are worthless and unlovable. You are way more than anything THAT MAN could ever say to you. Tell yourself daily how beautiful, smart and wise you are. You are the only person responsible for your joy and peace, so take it back from THAT MAN and never let another man make you doubt who you are or your abilities.

To Avoid Bipolar Brad, next time ask yourself:

1. Does he start a task and find it hard to finish it? Plan grand unrealistic projects (ex: rebuild the bathroom) and never finishes them?

Many women have come into my office and stated, "He tore out the stairs, he tore up the kitchen or he started a deck and it's been five months and our house is still a wreck!" Remember, Bipolar Brad has episodes of high and low energy and motivation. He may one day, while in a state of mania, tear out the kitchen cabinets, then go into a state of depression that persists for months. During that time, the project is sitting there uncompleted until his next manic phase, if at all. Sometimes Bipolar Brads will go from one project to another and leave several unfinished messes throughout your home or at his job.

2. Is he often irritable?

If you notice that he is quick to snap at you about any little thing, and you have to be concerned with his mood on a daily basis, you are probably dating a Bipolar Brad. Many men who are dealing with mental illness do not realize that their moods change from one minute to the next because this has been their state of mind their whole life. They often believe this behavior is normal. Therefore, it is important to begin to recognize what a "normal" day looks like for THAT MAN and begin to try and identify if he is moody or not.

3. Does he talk very quickly at times?

Many people with mental health issues often have rapid speech. Their thoughts are going so quickly that they cannot get them out of their head fast enough. Bipolar Brads often have great ideas and make great plans but rarely do they have the stick-to-itiveness to follow through with the plan to the end. This is because they cannot remain focused enough to sit down and create a plan of action for any one of the ideas that have come to mind.

4. Is he impulsive?

I have had women come into the office and tell me, "He went out and bought a boat, motorcycle or an expensive electronic item." He did this without consulting her and often paid for it with money from her account. Usually THAT MAN will say he deserved to do such things because he has been working so hard. Beware if your man is buying electronic toys or big money items for himself and putting you into financial ruin. Most Bipolar Brads do have emotional spending problems. These men buy these items thinking they will make them feel better, but they never do. Therefore, these men have to buy more and more expensive toys to try and get the "emotional "fix."

5. Does he sleep some weeks for more than eight hours and other weeks for less than four hours?

Bipolar Brads often have irregular sleep patterns, and not because they work a third shift job, either. Bipolar Brad's sleep issue comes from the chemical imbalance in his brain. There may be times when he sleeps nine to twelve hours and takes naps during the day, and others when he gets less than four hours total. When he is sleeping a lot he is usually in a depressed phase and when he is sleeping a little he is usually in a manic phase.

Again, these two phases will also be accompanied by other differing behaviors. For example, when THAT MAN is in a manic phase he will have rapid speech, engage in risky behaviors and display emotional spending. When THAT MAN is in a   phase, he will have an irregular sleep pattern but sleep more than ten hours a day; he will also be very irritable and angry and sometimes have suicidal thoughts.

What to do if you believe you are dating a man with mental illness

First and foremost, please approach this subject with him carefully, if you choose to do so at all. Most men do not receive this type of information or conversation well. Next, I recommend that you find a therapist to talk with about the situation. It will be very important to hear from a professional regarding your concerns. When you are looking for a professional, please seek out someone who specializes in the type of mental illness you believe your boyfriend/husband to be battling. Finally, consult with his family and close friends about his recent behaviors. The people closest to him may have witnessed some of these behaviors and could be very helpful to you when trying to decide your next steps.

Ray or Rachel (The Down-Low Man)

"I am embarrassed to say why I am here today, Dr. Thomas. My husband was caught in the park with another man last week. I had the embarrassing job of going downtown to bail him out of jail. How do I tell my children that their father is gay?"

Many women have heard stories about "down-low" men. These stories are shocking and cause women to become fearful about their own men being gay or bisexual.

It is difficult enough to be in love with a man who cheats on you with a woman. But, when THAT MAN comes home and says he is leaving you for a man, it takes hurt and pain to a deeper level. I have worked with women whose friends took them to gay clubs so they could see their men engaging in this behavior with their own eyes. I have also worked with women who received calls from their man's male lovers.

However, you find out, it is a shocking experience. Depending on the level of hurt and the amount of fear that you have of dating, it could take up to two years for you to regain your faith in men and intimate relationships.

There are two types of down-low men I have heard women discuss: Type One is the man who comes across as extremely manly and Type Two is the man who loves to play dress-up in your makeup and jewelry as a form of foreplay.

The Type One man is very concerned with his physical appearance. He is often meticulous about his clothing and keeps his hair and nails well-groomed. I have been told that Type One men are also obsessed with working out and being physically fit. Just as a woman is in competition with other women to get a man, these men are continually working their bodies because they are in competition to get other men. They are obsessed with their looks because they are trying to be "the number one pick" at the gay bars, yet at the same time they are anxious to hide the fact that they are on the down-low.

The wives or girlfriends of Type One may describe their relationship this way:

He is never here. He comes home from work, takes a shower, and goes to the gym for two hours. He comes home, takes another shower, and then tells me he is going out with the boys to the bar. He usually doesn't get home until five o'clock in the morning. Sometimes he doesn't come home at all.

After six months of this behavior, you began to realize that he is spending more time with his male friends than with you. Ultimately, you realize he is spending two or three days away from home each week. This may be okay if he were inviting you to join them, and they had other women present, but this is not the case.

You also need to be concerned if THAT MAN continually states how much he hates gay men and/or protests against the gay lifestyle. He may say things like, "Real men would never be gay." He may even speak about violently harming gay men. These gay-bashing comments are made in an effort to divert attention away from himself.

The Type Two Down-Low male is easier to recognize. These men are flamboyant, wearing flashy jewelry, fancy coats, tight skinny jeans and studded belts, or engage in other typically feminine behaviors.

One girlfriend of a Type Two Down-Low said:

Last week I was cleaning out the car and I found some clear nail polish, eyelashes and a bottle of perfume. A month ago, I found some panties and a bra stuffed in the backseat cushion. I was very upset and confronted my boyfriend because I thought he was cheating on me. I was really shocked when he told me he was a crossdresser and bisexual, and that those were his items.

You should be concerned if you find your man is purchasing clothing that looks unisex in nature. Also, be concerned if his style and color choices become more feminine. Other concerns include drastic changes in his friends, the community he frequents, and an increase in secrecy about his life. If THAT MAN begins to hang out with a new group of friends and he is unwilling to tell you where he met these people, then you should be cautious.

Type Two Down-Low males are very attentive and romantic. These men know the right words to say and put all the right moves on women, because they study women. They study her physical appearance, what she likes to wear, her hair, clothing type, and even her shoes. Like Type Ones, a Type Two man is usually secretive about his sexual identity/orientation, and may even purchase his woman's clothing, shoes, et cetera in the hopes that it will keep her from figuring it out.

A Type Two man may also be overly romantic in bed. He may want to paint your toes, shampoo your hair, or give you a full-body massage with body oil. That sounds lovely, doesn't it? It is, but not coming from the Down-Low male. These thoughtful acts are intended for the Type Two male to learn more about being female. He then takes the information and utilizes it in his gay relationship.

The significant other of a Type Two Down-Low man said:

I never realized that all the questions he asked me about the different perfumes were to help him with his research, to prepare him for romantic encounters with other men. He often asked me about different nightgowns and talked to me about how I felt when I wore a lace night gown as opposed to a satin one.

One night I came home and found him wearing my satin pajamas and spraying my perfume. He said he just loved the way they felt on his skin. He then began to act silly, and I thought nothing of it until I came home two weeks later and found him wearing my pajamas and smelling like my perfume again.

INFECTION AND THE DOWN-LOW MALE

Women involved with Down-Low men often contract bacterial infections and inflammation of the uterus. These issues come about because these men may have penetrated another man anally, then went home and penetrated her vaginally.

The infection comes from fecal material. When you keep contracting bacterial infections or have inflammation of the uterus over and over again, go see a doctor. Initially, the doctor's diagnosis makes no sense to you. You are confused because the doctor tells you that there is fecal matter in the swab, and begins to explain to you how this could have happened.

At this point you begin to question the relationship. The next step is for you to leave the relationship, get tested and seek help from a therapist to get over the psychological pain that has been inflicted on you.

When the man you love is in love with another man, it really damages your ego and self-esteem. You feel flooded with emotions such as anger, fear, embarrassment, shame and thoughts that you are stupid for not figuring it out earlier. And when a man leaves you for another man, you may think, "What is it about me that would cause him to turn to a man?"

You have to understand that your man's sexual preference has nothing to do with your ability or inability to satisfy him. Therefore, you must not allow negative thoughts, such as your not being "woman enough" to please him, to fill your mind.

PROTECTING HIS IMAGE

Many men who are on the "down-low" have two images they allow others to see: their true self and their acceptable self. To protect these images, men have projected their blame, shame or guilt onto the women in the relationship.

I have heard some men tell their girlfriend or wife, "You are the reason I'm gay!" This is a lie. No woman can be the reason for a man turning to another man for love, just like no woman, no matter how fabulous, cannot make a gay man straight.

Also understand that you had nothing to do with THAT MAN creating a false acceptable self. The acceptable self is his protection from the judgment of the world. It allows him to mask his true self and what he really wants to do, and that is to be openly gay. It has nothing to do with you, so seek the help you need to in order to drop the guilt, shame and or guilt and move on.

WARNING SIGNS

The Down-Low man has lied so many times about his whereabouts, friends and lifestyle that you may become confused as to what is truly manly behavior and what is not. Therefore, I'm sharing with you some behaviors and warning signs that a man may be on the "down low."

If you have been in the relationship for more than six months and he has never tried to consummate the relationship, he may be on the "down low." Some men are celibate due to personal preference or religious reasons. These gentlemen are not the men being referred to in this chapter.

The men we're talking about here are those who openly tell you they are attracted to you but usually do not display their affection towards you. These men appear emotionally detached from you the majority of the time.

Often you wonder, "What am I doing here?" He rarely notices changes in clothing or hairstyle. A down-low brother may rarely initiate intimacy or sex with you as well.

If a man has married you but continually doesn't initiate sex or avoids sex with you altogether, he may not be attracted to you. It may be that this man needs to have the appearance of a heterosexual relationship for some reason. Some men who are in male-dominated fields know that same-sex relationships are frowned upon and therefore need the appearance of being married with kids for their positions to remain intact.

Some women I've worked with tell me their husbands only show interest in sex every once in a while, sometimes just once or twice a month. A healthy sexual relationship inside of marriage usually consists of making love at least once a week.

Couples who have been married less than three years should be making love an average of two to three times a week. I have worked with numerous women who say to me, "Dr. Thomas, I have passed him naked, put on sexy lingerie and he won't even look at me."

Some have told me they would walk into the room wearing a beautiful new teddy, and he would just look up and say, "Oh that's nice," and return to whatever he had been doing before, as if he didn't recognize this was her way of saying, "Let's make love tonight."

There are other possible reasons for this reaction, such as he has some undiagnosed health issues; he is cheating with another woman; or he is depressed. However, if a woman continually tries to be romantic and THAT MAN doesn't acknowledge her efforts, he might indeed be on the down-low.

For men, sexual arousal is very visually oriented. No man who is into women can resist a woman who is standing in front of him naked. All women have the ability to seduce, tempt and attract heterosexual men. So, when a man resists or ignores the woman he is with or doesn't find her attractive at all anymore but isn't willing to leave the relationship, he might have something else on the side.

Ladies, be aware that down-low men are not always easy to spot. I have found some women believe they can spot a down-low man a mile away. I used to think that too.

In college, there was a very popular fraternity guy. He was also an athlete and a "pretty boy," and every woman on campus adored him.

Imagine their shock twenty years later when the sorority girls learned that this man who was so handsome, charming, masculine, and buff was on the down-low, and had recently come out as gay. His actions, attire and womanizing gave him the appearance of a straight male.

Many women think they can "pick out" the gay ones or identify the down-low ones. It's sometimes impossible to tell if a person is straight or gay by looking at them. The same is especially true of Down-Low men, so stop trying.

To avoid the Down-Low male next time, ask yourself:

1. Is he vain and arrogant?

Does THAT MAN take longer than you to get dressed to go out for the evening? Does he go to the spa more than you for facials, manicures and pedicures? Or, does he spend a lot of time taking selfies and posting them on all of his social media accounts? Some down-low men are very vain and into pampering themselves more than women. If he is constantly talking about how everyone wants him or desires him for his looks, fashions sense or cologne, he is vain and may be on the down-low.

2. Does he often brag about his numerous exotic sexual experiences?

Some down-low men constantly brag about the different sexual encounters they have had and the numerous outlandish things they have done in the bedroom with other people. If a woman asks him specifically, "Do you have sex with men?" he may say no, though some Down-Low men are honest about it. These men believe if they are "givers" and not "receivers" they are not gay. Sometimes down-low men will even refer to themselves as bisexual or just "nasty." You have to ask sexual history questions of down-low men and not be afraid if they become upset or offended. I have worked with some down-low men, and one thing I learned is if the woman does not ask the right questions about their past sexual history they won't mention the threesomes with both men and women or the sex parties they attend that include sleeping with other men.

If you believe your man is on the down-low do not be afraid to say, "I have some questions and I hope I do not offend you but I need to get these questions answered before we go any further." And, ladies, if you still think in your heart that THAT MAN is on the down-low, please DO NOT have unprotected sex with him for any reason at all.

3. Was he incarcerated for a long period of time?

Some men who have been in prison for several years learned how to survive by becoming the female in the relationship. It provides them protection from others on the inside. This behavior is very common in prison and when men leave prison they do not consider their behavior as being gay. These men believe it was a survival instinct.

The down-low men I have worked with often told me that in order to survive in prison they did a lot of things that they regret and would take to the grave. I can understand learning and adapting to an environment especially one so dangerous; that said, I also believe that the learned behavior stays deeply embedded inside of THAT MAN's mind and creates a sexual appetite for the behavior over time. Therefore, what was once a survival technique inside of the prison becomes a desire outside. Some of these men do not like the fact that now they desire relationships with men and women but they do not know how to stop their cravings. These are the men who will come into therapy and say, "I need help" when they no longer want to live a double life. Also, there are men who will say, "I am here because I realize now that I am gay and I need to get out of the heterosexual relationship that I am in presently."

This is a difficult road for a man to manage, but in time each man I have worked with has learned how to overcome this dilemma and move forward with his sexual identity. For the woman who is involved with a gentleman who was recently released from prison, the sexual history questions are paramount!

In conclusion, stay patient in the dating process and look for warning signs of down-low men. Warning signs are always there, but some women ignore the signs to avoid being alone in life. Loneliness is not such a horrible thing when one thinks of the devastation that follows finding out that your man is on the down-low.

Womanizing Wayne (The Sexually Addicted Man)

"Dr. Thomas, yesterday my husband came home from a work trip and I was preparing to wash his clothes. Our eleven-year-old son often asked me if he could help unpack his dad's suitcase. I was very embarrassed when our son came to me and said, "Mom, why does Dad have condoms in his suitcase? You two are married, right? So why does he have condoms?"

Many people deal with this type of man. Womanizing Wayne has been in the life of nearly every woman I know, including my own. This is usually a very attractive guy, and he knows it and uses it to his advantage. He uses his looks and his abilities to prey on women and manipulate them into giving him what he wants.

Womanizing Wayne can sweet talk you all day long. Ladies, stop going for the "cute guy." Start looking for more than a handsome face. These guys are constantly on the prowl, looking for other women they can date. Wayne is never happy with just one woman.

I have counseled a lot of Waynes, most of them under thirty-eight years old. They tell me, "I don't plan on settling down until I am forty."

They are attractive, smart, educated and believe they are a hot commodity because of this. These guys even go around saying to themselves, "I know I look good so I don't need a woman to tell me."

The sad truth is most of these men are in pain and are using sex as a way to "self-medicate." So, if you have thought, "What is wrong with me?" or "Why does he continue to do this to me?" the truth is, it's not you. It's him. He is ill and needs professional help.

That said, he will likely never get the help he needs because he is addicted to the rush he gets from pursuing and conquering women. These men are sex addicts. No one wants to talk about it or call it what it is — an inappropriate way of coping with their pain. Instead, they end up hurting the women they claim to love because they will not get treated for their illness.

The Sexually Addicted man will be very secretive. He will have numerous passwords on his cell phone, laptop, television, and email accounts. He may have two or three cell phones, one you know of and the other(s) stashed away in the garage, in the trunk of the car, in his desk at work, or at a friend's house. The same holds true for his social media accounts. He will have one under his birth name and others under nicknames or another name that you know nothing about.

Also, he will constantly want to go places without you. For example, you have a gym membership together but you can never go together because the other women he entertains work out at the same gym. Another ploy is, he only wants to go to the gym early — five or six a.m. — or really late — ten to eleven p.m., times most people are sleeping. If you haven't figured it out, it's because he's not going to the gym at all. He is meeting the other girl there and leaving the gym to take her to the movies, dinner, breakfast or something else.

He might also say, "I'm going to Kroger, Walmart, Sam's," et cetera late at night or early in the morning and doesn't want you to go with him. Don't be fooled by the "You have to stay home with the kids" thing either.

You wouldn't have to stay home with the kids if he were willing to go during normal hours like other families do.

Often these men come home and tell you about the women who hit on them and how they did not respond, to make you feel "proud" of him. That is really his illness acting up. A Sexually Addicted man feeds off being seen, heard and the center of attention. If you find he always has to be the life of the party and he is attracting attention wherever you go, beware.

Sexually Addicted men are constantly flirting with women, even in your presence. Let's say the two of you go to a restaurant. While you are eating your meal a group of women sits down nearby and he begins to comment on something about one of them.

For example, he may say, "That's a cool hairstyle. How did you get it like that?" It seems innocent enough, right? No, this is his way of being seen again. He will continue talking with this woman as if he is really interested, but it is just a way to feed into his need for attention.

The Waynes of the world also will make you feel very special all the time. He may take you to a nice restaurant, buy you flowers and sing to you all day long. But when it's time for him to commit to you in a relationship he has a million reasons why it's impossible to do. He may say, "Girl, you know I love you but I'm too young. I haven't completed my degree or my child support's too high. But when it goes down I can afford a ring."

Waynes continually make you feel special, especially when they get caught cheating. Ladies, if he says, "I will never do it again" but this is your third or fourth time busting him, he WILL do it again.

Men with this mindset don't stop without professional intervention. They do not understand why they do what they do and we as women have to stop trying to figure it out for them.

Are you constantly asking yourself, "What can I do to change him or help him?" This is not your responsibility. I have had women in sessions say to me, "I know he fathered two different children by two different women inside our relationship, but I love him." We then have to shift the discussion to why do you as a woman believe it is okay for him to continually sexually abuse you.

Yes, I said sexual abuse. When a man sleeps around and doesn't use protection, he is sexually abusing you. How? He is abusing you because he is putting you at risk for HIV and sexually transmitted diseases each time he sleeps with that other woman. Hopefully, you are using a condom with him. I know some women who tell me because they have been seeing THAT MAN for some time they have stopped using condoms. Ladies, be smart. If he isn't your husband and you suspect he's playing around,, use a condom. Shoot, even if he *is* your husband you may need to use a condom. There are married womanizers out there too.

I know that because I have had to counsel their wives regarding protecting themselves from further STDs and bacterial infections. We love our men and want to believe they would protect us from infection, but we must face the fact that some of them don't care enough about protecting us or even their own lives.

Womanizing Wayne is only concerned with his next sexual high. This obsession causes him to say, "Who cares about a condom?" He just wants to feel good instantly and these sexual urges cause him to not think rationally.

If your former man fathered two children by two different women while he was in a relationship with you, ask yourself these two questions: What was it about him that had me hooked and why did I stay so long? Once you figure out this answer, you will not allow future Waynes to be in your life.

As a woman who has dated a Wayne in the past, I can tell you the best thing to do is to stop dating for at least a period of four months so you can clear your head, heal your heart and regain your identity. I will explain this more in detail in section two. The goal of taking a respite from men is to help you regain your clarity in a relationship. The longer you were with THAT MAN, the longer you will need to recover from THAT MAN.

Of all the types of men in this book, Womanizing Waynes have the potential to mess up women's minds the most because they are beautiful, smart, charming; plus, for some of you, it is the best sex you have ever had. So I understand when women come into my office sick to their stomach because of "Womanizing Wayne." Most women think Wayne is the man she is going to marry. This man has the total package, and generally the woman's family loves him too.

Another way to identify a Wayne is by the number of "female friends" he has around him. Some of the women THAT MAN hangs out with are legitimate friends, but with others he uses the term "friend" as a cover. It's sad that these women usually know you are his girlfriend and they don't mind being in second position or being the woman on the side. I will discuss the issues these women have in the next section too.

If you are a woman on the side, please stop it, because eventually what you have done to someone else will be done to you. It is the law of reciprocity. In other words, you will reap what you have sown.

Let's review. If you are dealing with a man who: (a) has multiple female friends, (b) constantly cheats on you, (c) has locked cell phones, emails, and hangs out late in stores and you cannot go with him, you probably have a Womanizing Wayne in your life. Think about these warning signs. There are numerous others but these are the signs that have shown up often in my practice.

Remember, Womanizing Wayne never has only one woman. He is too insecure for that. He has to always have a side piece, just in case the one he is with "messes up."

Finally, know that sometimes a Wayne will say, "She and I broke up." Ask him to prove it. This may mean you have to call the other woman and hear it from her mouth. However, be warned: If this woman is a side piece she will say anything for him. If he doesn't want to prove it, then leave him alone.

He cannot mistreat you unless you allow it. Tell yourself that you deserve all the man or no man at all. You are worth it. If you don't believe you are worth it, seek out professional help so you and your therapist can get you to personal wholeness before you ever deal with another man.

Signs you are dealing with Womanizing Wayne:

1. He refuses to take you out in public, but calls you his woman.

Let's say a woman plans to attend a concert with Womanizing Wayne and buys the tickets months in advance. He says, "Yeah, we are going," but the day of the concert he complains of being tired and not feeling well.

The woman begins to notice that over the last six months he has not taken her out in public at all. She begins to wonder if there is another woman.

Womanizing Wayne will constantly make a woman question herself and believe that she has issues, when really she has no issues at all. The issues are with him and the woman has been exposed to his addiction for so long that she begins to think she is the problem.

You need to go with your initial feeling about what is going on here and make a decision about what to do. Do not wait too long or you will talk yourself out of doing what is truly best for you. It may be that little girl with Daddy Damage inside of you who is telling you to, "Be nice and a little more patient with him and he will change."

2. Does he constantly bring up his old girlfriend with you as if he's reliving the past?

Does That Man start talking about a relationship he had five or ten years ago as if it just happened? He may start out by saying, "I once dated a girl who," or "I remember Tonya, man, she was fine, her body was banging!" If you're with a man who constantly wants to relive his past relationships with you, he is a Womanizing Wayne.

3. Does he view pornography numerous times a week? Or, does he prefer to watch pornography over lovemaking with you?

Viewing porn excessively actually changes a man's brainwaves, to the point where he finds less pleasure in connecting with a woman and more pleasure in pleasuring himself. Therefore, his need for intimate, body-to-body contact decreases while his impulse for immediate gratification increases. Ultimately, this man will not find pleasure in sex with a woman unless she is considered exotic or forbidden (a stripper, prostitute, or someone's wife).

4. Does he frequent strip clubs, prostitutes or chat lines regularly?

If THAT MAN is spending more time in gentlemen's clubs or on chat lines, he is more than likely sex addicted. Some warning signs are high phone bills, spending money on hotels excessively or when it's not warranted (i.e., he is not traveling for business), or his paycheck is gone after he returns home from hanging out with his friends. If THAT MAN asks you to do perform weird sexual acts or dress in certain ways only, he may also be dealing with some form of sexual addiction.

5. Does he criticize you sexually?

If the guy you are dating constantly compares you sexually to other women he has dated you, have a problem. If he says, "You don't do (fill in the blank) like Kim and you need to work on that, then you are dealing with a Womanizing Wayne.

Why would you try to be like anyone else but yourself? If Kim was so great, he would still be with her. Or maybe Kim got smart and walked away.

You do not need criticism about your sexual performance. This leads to thoughts of "Maybe I'm bad in bed" and lowers your self-esteem.

This emotional pain and self-doubt can even cause negative physical reactions like vaginal dryness and pain during intercourse. Finally, your sex drive can disappear altogether, all because THAT MAN put negative thoughts in your mind about your ability to fulfill him sexually.

Part Two
Reclaiming Your Mind, Body and Spirit Now That You Have Left *THAT MAN*

Grieving the Relationship

Dealing with the pain of a hurtful relationship can be difficult and take some time. Trust me, I know. We all know. All of us have had at least one relationship that took us through the wringer and caused us to hit a very low point in life. Now that you are aware of the different types of unhealthy men you have dated, you hopefully are going to or have already left that relationship. It is now time for you to grieve and begin your healing process.

Some women cannot eat, sleep, think when they are leaving a relationship; some probably had some type of diarrhea or nausea as well. See, when you grieve a relationship, your body goes through a detoxification process. How else will you get better if you don't allow your body time to purge all of the "dis-ease" THAT MAN put you through? Just like your relationship took time to establish, your recovery process will take time as well.

Remember your first love? He was cute, smart, funny, smelled good, had a beautiful smile; he may even have taken your virginity. You loved him so much. What was it like when he broke up with you, or you broke up with him? Remember the nights that you cried, the days you could not eat? The number of times you tried to call him or thought about getting back with him but your girlfriend talked you out of it?

How long did this process last? Two or three weeks? One day? One month? Well, however long it was, that was your natural grief cycle. If you ever experience heartbreak again, you will know how long you will need to be alone before you enter into another relationship. The alone time allows you an opportunity to refocus your identity and regain your sanity.

We all have a relationship grief cycle before we move on and, ladies, you need to know exactly what yours is. If you have ever lost a loved one or a pet, ended another relationship and felt horrible for a period of time, you know what I mean. Some people grieve for two weeks. For others, it may be two months. Once you know your grief cycle, you will be able to make it through that time period without feeling like you are going to lose your mind.

One more thing to note, if you have been with that person for more than a year, it could take you up to half that time to recover. THAT MAN. Therefore, if you were in the relationship for one year, you may need six months to process out your thoughts, emotions, and actions from the impact of the relationship. The least amount of time is about four months. Give yourself this time. Don't jump into another relationship too fast, thinking, "It will help me get over him." It won't. It will push your pain down and your relationship recovery time will be longer. The key is to know yourself and realize when you are healed.

When you have been in a relationship for more than six months, sometimes you may lose your identity and take on his. This happens when much of what you do is centered on his wants and dreams. This chasing of his dreams causes you to put your own on hold or even forget about them because they appear to be out of reach.

Some women believe there is now no time for their passions in life. This is why every woman must take a sabbatical from dating so she can ask herself, "Now, who am I and what do I want for me?" Hopefully, once you answer the questions above, you will begin your journey to having life become grand after THAT MAN.

What Did You Learn From Him?

Believe it or not, we all learn something from every relationship we have been in — whether it's positive or not. Whatever it is, intimate or not, we take bits and pieces from those people who have been a part of our lives, even if it's just a small period of time. So begin to think about the things you gained from this experience.

First, ask yourself, "What was the most meaningful thing that happened while I was with this guy?" This may take you some time to figure out.

There are times in our lives when we have to think about meaning. Meaning is what you gain and what you can use to help you become more productive in the future.

It is important to remember that the relationship wasn't all bad. It may feel like it was, but it was not. So start to think about the good qualities he had and the things you enjoyed about him. These may be things that attracted you to him in the beginning.

Get a piece of paper and begin to write them down. Some things that you learned are invaluable. They may be things like, "I learned I like walks in the park," or "I learned I like roller skating."

A lot of what you learned from him are things that maybe you had not gotten in the past or had never experienced before. Of course, ladies, we all know that when you learn good things you also learn bad things. So you need to list these as well.

Writing down what you learned, both positive and negative, will start your healing process. Sometimes you will forget that even though the relationship is over, he did teach you some good things that will be tools to use in the next relationship. This includes characteristics you liked about him and would like to see in other men you date.

Each time you enter a new relationship you should take what you learned from the old one and apply it. Make this a habit. You will be well pleased with how you are attracting men who are more attentive to your needs.

This activity will also allow you to learn more about what you like and desire in a man. Most of the time women do not seek out qualities they like, other than the physical ones, and end up missing out on a lot of good men.

Daddy Damage

Last week I was watching "Are We There Yet?" with my children. I recall the scene where the son was sitting on the front porch with his bags packed waiting for his father to show up. His sister said to him, "He's not coming; I told you he's not coming!"

Their father had repeatedly told them on different occasions that he would pick them up for the weekend, only to fail to show up. The girl was the older of the two children and she had come to realize that her father was full of lies and broken promises, while her brother still longed and hoped for the day that his father would honor his word. This situation is an experience many children know all too well. As mentioned previously, experiences like this one are what I call "Daddy Damage."

Daddy Damage consists of different situations that happen in a young girl's life that cause her to have issues in her intimate relationships with men. I know that there are numerous healthy fathers in the world, and we love and applaud them for raising healthy young women. I am not talking about those fathers In this chapter, I will only focus on the fathers that cause Daddy Damage, along with tips to help women overcome it.

As I said previously, Daddy Damage starts in early childhood, when a little girl is excited about her daddy and loves him dearly, but he begins to disappoint her. These little girls are yearning for love that their fathers are not able to or refuse to give to them. They are disappointed so often that they get used to all the excuses and false promises, yet continue to believe their fathers will keep their word the next time. Eventually, they even start making their own excuses for their fathers' poor behavior.

Sound familiar? This is the same process that adult women go through in unhealthy relationships with men like Bipolar Brad. These women are continually on an emotional rollercoaster and do not understand how to get off, because they have dealt with this behavior all of their childhood.

Daddy Damage can affect a woman in a number of ways. One way is emotional abuse — f he damaged her emotionally when he continually failed to show up for events or made promises to spend time with her and never did. He set her up for failure in relationships by having her believe that he would come and that he would "change."

As little girls we are taught to be patient, nice, share and don't be mean to others; meanwhile boys are taught to take what they want, be rough, don't care and "better not cry." Girls are socialized very differently from boys and many times girls accept too much in both intimate and personal relationships before they say enough is enough.

Having this type of dad creates an issue of rejection and abandonment in women (I will go into this in more detail in the next section). It may cause women to go out looking for men who will never leave them. This woman finds her worth in what men will say to her or do for her. This woman is looking to another man to heal the Daddy Damage she has experienced. The only problem is THAT MAN didn't do the damage therefore he cannot fix it. Her father is responsible for the damage and he can help her recover from it. If not her father, she can still experience healing and emotional health with the help of a therapist, counselor or pastor.

Over the years I have noticed four different categories of Daddy Damage: Deadbeat Daddy, Demoralizing Daddy, Depressed Daddy and Dowry Daddy.

Deadbeat Daddy (Absent)

The Deadbeat Daddy is very familiar to a lot of people, either through personal experience or because we have heard about him over the years. This is the absentee father, the one who knows he has a child but doesn't take part in his or her life at all. In some cases he has never even seen the child.

This is the father who doesn't pay child support and believes, "The government has no right in his business." This is the man who if his daughter's mother finds out he has a new job, has gotten a pay raise, or he has picked up a second job, may quit the job, not take the raise or even lie about his address to get out of paying child support. While Deadbeat Daddy can cause damage to both his sons and daughters, for our purposes we're going to focus on the girls.

The Daddy Damage begins as the young girl grows and hears the stories from her mother or family members about her father's behavior, When a father doesn't want to be involved in his daughter's life and she knows it, she starts looking for someone to fill in the void. After years of hearing, seeing and experiencing the rejection from her father, she now wants to find someone to love her. Also, when the father isn't around the young girl has no one to educate her about boys or their behaviors. This may lead to her accepting all types of guys' invitations for a date. Her mother, friends and family members can see that the men she dates are unhealthy; however, she cannot see it because she believes if she continues to be patient in the relationship everything will work itself out.

A father who is a deadbeat communicates to his daughter that she is not worthy of his love, time or energy. Therefore, she goes around trying to prove to herself and everyone else that she is worthy of these things. This ultimately leads to her connecting with a man or many men who do not appreciate her. She may even connect to men who continue to abandon her the same way her father did when she was a little girl. To break the cycle, this woman must begin to value herself and believe she is worthy to be loved.

Demoralizing Daddy (Abusive)

The next type of Daddy Damage comes from the demoralizing father. This father has physically, sexually, verbally, mentally or emotionally abused his daughter.

This man has no morals at all. He takes advantage of his daughter without thinking twice about it. These include the fathers who, either high/drunk or sober, and call their daughter into the bedroom to dance for them, have sex with them or even watch him have sex with another woman or man. Some men even sell their daughters for sex or drugs.

I have talked with numerous women who learned about sex from their fathers, and not in a good way. The Demoralizing Daddy continually causes his daughter to think she is doing something bad and therefore deserves the abuse.

Women who have had demoralizing fathers often say, "I am so ashamed of what I did." Or "I can't believe that I liked it and began to look forward to it." Sometimes these daughters begin to look at their fathers as their boyfriends and even resented their mothers.

If you are reading this book and this is your story, don't carry around blame, shame and guilt from what your father did to you. He was immoral and a monster. You were the daughter he was supposed to protect from evil, but instead he *was* the evil. The fact that you enjoyed it is not your fault either. Once anyone experiences sex, chemicals in our brain cause us to want to experience it again and again. Your body was simply doing what it was naturally designed to do.

Finally, for those of you who resented your mother and even had thoughts of harming her, please forgive yourself. You were made to believe that you were in a healthy loving relationship and, like anyone else, wanted to protect what was yours.

A Demoralizing Daddy can cause a daughter to become over-sexualized, mentally ill, a lesbian or even violent. The over-sexualized daughter is the girl in school that everyone knows for sleeping around. She may even have slept with her sister's boyfriends, best friends' boyfriends, or some of her college sorority sisters' men.

These women cannot understand why they enjoy sex so much and sometimes engage in behavior even they don't consider normal, such as making videos, stripping, engaging in prostitution, and having sex with multiple partners.

Some women I have counseled say, "I am only good at this stuff," or "No one likes me if I don't do these sex acts for them." The treatment goal with these women is to overcome the mental lie that your father put inside of your head and caused you to believe.

In my work with these women, it's not uncommon for me to hear, "A penis is nasty, dirty, and ugly, I will never have another one of those close to me again." In their mind the penis is bad, not the person. Therefore these young girls grow up to hate the penis and therefore believe they cannot be in a relationship with a male because he has one.

Some teenage girls that I have worked with have even stated, "I don't know how to do boys but I know how to do girls." Meaning, "I feel comfortable/safe in relationships with girls, not boys."

These women have responded to their Daddy Damage in a way that makes all men evil, nasty, and dirty. This is just not true. There are a lot of good men in the world and these men are also looking for good women.

If this is you, it's important to understand that your daddy violated you. Your daddy was sick, not his penis. The penis was just the tool he used to commit the violent, nasty act of sexual abuse against you. You may have had to perform oral sex on your demoralizing daddy. You said in your mind, "This penis is bad, this is bad and I am bad." In actuality, the penis isn't bad, you were not bad and if the oral sex had been performed on someone you choose to love and perform it on willingly, you would not be thinking about it in this way.

For those women who are lesbians and believe, "I can't do men because all penises are bad," know that this belief is the result of the horrifying abuse you endured. This is an understandable reaction, especially if you've never had a healthy sexual experience with a man, but it's simply not true.

Now is the time to stop accepting the lie. Not all men are horrible and not all penises are bad, dirty and sick, and a healthy lovemaking experience between a man and a woman is a good thing. The old saying "Don't knock it until you try it" may apply here.

Mental illness can also develop as a result of dealing with Demoralizing Daddy. Girls who are repeatedly molested or physically abused by their fathers have a difficult time dealing with the dichotomy of love-hate. They hate what he did to them, yet the child inside may still love him. For some, the mind cannot handle the repetitive thoughts and mixed emotions, especially if the abuse has gone on for a long period of time. The mind therefore creates little compartments within itself to protect itself from total destruction. In some cases these women develop mild depression, while others develop schizophrenia or other severe conditions, including Dissociative Identity Disorder, where they create a separate personality.

Or, the brain may shut down totally (go into shock) and create a separate area in the mind in which it stores all of the information from the traumatic experience. It becomes locked away and she literally does not remember it happening. In this case, the woman may experience a whole host of problems in her life and not understand why, until the memories or triggered and/or her issues are dealt with in therapy.

Lastly, a Demoralizing Daddy can create a violent streak in a woman. Some women become so angry about the violation and different forms of abuse that they allow anger to grow and take hold of the mind and spirit.

This is the woman about which everyone says, "Man, she is so mean"; "She is never happy."; "She is always negative and has a bad attitude"; or "She hates." This is the woman to whom guys say, "You are hard to please or you are too nasty and I just can't take all your judgment and criticism anymore."

What has happened to this woman is what I call Daddy Anger Damage. She says, "My daddy hurt me but one else ever will." This really means that she will not allow anyone else — not a friend, family member, boyfriend, or even her children — to get close to her, because she is afraid to trust another person who could hurt her again.

She then begins to build invisible walls around her heart to protect herself. It means she must be mean to all of the people she cares about to keep them at arm's length. What she really wants is to have longstanding, trusting relationships, but she is so fearful that her trust will be violated again that she continued to push them away.

This causes her to appear cold, mean, and angry to everyone she meets. Sometimes she may even walk around with a permanent mean look on her face because she has had a negative disposition and attitude for so long. Over time, the years of anger and hurt can show up physically in your body as well.

Some women who carry around Daddy Anger Damage get on a serious path of destruction. Sometimes this path begins in elementary school. These are the tough girls, bullies, and fighters that others are afraid of.

These girls grow up to become the women who fight their boyfriends, commit crimes and sometimes ultimately end up in prison, all because they had Daddy Damage that led to Daddy Anger Damage. This anger becomes an addiction and therefore very dangerous to herself and others.

Depressed Daddy (Mentally ill)

The Depressed Daddy is the father that is present in the home and wants to interact with his daughter but due to his own mental health challenges is unable to do so. Depression causes a person to be fatigued and have a lack of energy, among other things. Some common symptoms of depression in men include insomnia, anger, irritability, impulsiveness and overspending.

Depressed Daddy may play with his daughter one day, and the next ignore her. He may in one breath praise her for her abilities and in the next curse her out for no apparent reason. Or, Depending on Depressed Daddy's mood cycle, he may yell, scream and be verbally abusive to his daughter on a daily basis.

This is the house where everyone walks around on eggshells. The daughter may not want to invite friends over for fear that her dad may curse her out, hit on her friend, or be high on drugs or drunk. Most men battling depression will often use drugs or alcohol as a coping tool to help manage their depression. It is very nerve-wracking for his daughter to bring home friends because she is not sure what type of daddy she may encounter.

There is another other type of Depressed Daddy, one who refuses to interact with his daughter on a deep level simply because she is a girl. This man is sad because he wanted a son, and if he doesn't ignore her altogether he might dress her up as a boy and involve her in all sports that are masculine, such as basketball, flag football, soccer or softball. He may also take her to professional games, again, often dressing her like a boy. Activities that are feminine or female-oriented — like cheerleading, volleyball, or gymnastics — are totally out of the question.

This Depressed Daddy will only interact with his daughter on a surface level or when it comes to sports. If she asks him about anything feminine he begins to reject her and shut down the conversation, or redirect her to her mother. This type of talk is very uncomfortable to him because he really doesn't understand girls and women in that way.

The daughter of Depressed Daddy truly wants to get closer to her dad but comes to realize that he will push her away unless it's a subject of interest to him. So she becomes overly concerned with pleasing him, and does things to make her father happy instead of trying to make herself happy. This daughter also lives with constant anxiety because she does everything to get her dad's approval, but she cannot get it, no matter what. The Depressed Daddy will always find ways to push his daughter's affections away.

A woman who grows up with a Depressed Daddy may develop a Spirit of Rejection, which results from her father's inability to accept her for herself., and his repeated denial of her feminine side and desires. Or she may develop a mental illness called Borderline Personality Disorder. This disorder is rooted in manipulation and threats, which are formed from years of being denied true love and affection by her father. The young girl believes that she can only receive love by being deceitful and making threats to harm herself. Borderline Personality Disorder is one of the most difficult Daddy Damage issues to overcome.

Dowry Daddy (Financial)

This type of daddy believes his job is to provide financially for his daughter, and that is all. If he does so, in his mind, he is an excellent father. The Dowry Daddy typically does not live in the home with his daughter and makes it a point to send the checks on time; however, when it comes to emotional support he runs in and out of her life.

This type of father not only meets all his financial goals, he also tries to buy his daughter's affections. The Dowry Daddy typically only comes around on birthdays, holidays, and occasionally for no apparent reason except to give his daughter some money. He believes this makes him the perfect father and he wears it like a badge of honor.

The Dowry Daddy also prides himself on the lavish gifts he can buy his daughter. She is the little girl who always has her hair and nails done. She has the latest fashionable clothing and electronic items to go with it. As she gets older, he purchases bigger items like cars and expensive jewelry; establish a trust for her; and pay her college tuition. What he doesn't realize is that his daughter needs his time, love and affection as well, and that she would gladly give the gifts away for some quality time with him.

Dowry Daddy creates three different issues for his daughter: abandonment issues, bipolar disorder, and "gold digger" syndrome. Abandonment issues arise from the lack of regular interaction with her father. Abandonment is when a child is left behind, forsaken or deserted by a parent. Being repeatedly forsaken by her father creates concerns in the young woman's mind about future intimate relationships and whether a man will stay with her.

She begins to do things that go above and beyond her call as a girlfriend to keep the man. For example, she may pay his bills, participate in unhealthy sexual acts with him and others, or she may have a child to try to keep him connected to her.

Women who develop bipolar disorder have an even deeper level of emotional and mental trauma. As mentioned earlier, this disorder causes people to constantly vacillate between two emotional extremes, hence the terms "bi" which means two and "polar" which signifies opposites. Some days these women are happy and others she is sad or angry, often without knowing why.

Her father's constant abandonment helped create these mood swings. The constant uncertainty of her father's love makes it difficult for her to feel secure in other relationships. This creates mental stress and anguish because she's constantly afraid of being abandoned again. Her fear, joy and sadness vacillate with the everchanging issues and uncertainties of the relationship.

Finally, a Dowry Daddy can create a spirit of greed and ungratefulness in his daughter, thus the Gold Digger Syndrome. This woman believes men are supposed to buy her everything she wants, whenever she wants it, because this is what her father used to do. Her man should do whatever it takes, even go into debt, to get her these things.

This mindset stems from Dowry Daddy continually buying his daughter's love over the years. His behavior created the belief that men are only good for meeting her material, emotional, mental or physical desires. She feels entitled to everything she asks for, and is willing to walk away from otherwise wonderful men if she doesn't get it.

The Dowry Daddy also creates emotional and mental unrest in his daughter's mind. The goal for this woman is to look at healthy relationships and begin to search within herself for her personal worth. She must understand that her value is not tied to the material items she possesses.

Hurt

Everyone knows that when you are displaying anger you have really been hurt as well. You cannot believe that you would love a man so hard, so deep, and with every bit of your breath and he could turn around and treat you so badly. This hurt makes you feel like less than nothing. You may have thoughts of suicide and sometimes homicide because this hurt is so overwhelming.

Hurt is heart-wrenching when it happens inside of a relationship where you allowed yourself to be open, transparent, and vulnerable. It takes a lot to trust a man and allow him into your heart, especially if you have Daddy Damage and/or broken trust experiences from previous relationships. As a woman, I understand that hurt can come over and over again in a relationship, but so does joy. For you to heal from hurt, you must begin to focus on the joy that has been in your life before THAT MAN and the recovery work you are doing after THAT MAN.

To effectively get over your hurt, you must understand your healing cycle. If you do not know your healing cycle, think about the last time you experienced hurt. Then ask yourself, what caused the hurt, how long it lasted (most of us experience it for at least two weeks), and where you felt it in your body. These are three of the beginning pieces to recovery from hurt.

High school is about the time we experience our first major relationship hurt, so this would be a good place to examine how long it lasted. A common example of this kind of hurt is when a girlfriend breaks your trust through gossip or by sleeping with your man.

Take yourself back to that time period and think about the hurt you felt; recall the emotions, close your eyes and get your senses involved. What do you see, smell, touch? Now, how long did you allow yourself to stay with the hurt?

The next piece is to understand who caused the hurt: a friend, lover, parent, or sibling? Again, think back and experience the moment. Did you cry a long time? Did your stomach hurt? Did you vomit? Did you have diarrhea?

The body reacts to hurt as well as to other strong emotions. To heal from hurt, it is important to let it go. Put it back into the past you took it from. No longer do you have to say, "Back in eleventh grade Kim told everyone I had an abortion or Kim stole my boyfriend." Kim has probably moved on with her life and forgot all about the incident you are still hurting over.

Now it is time for you to move on with your life as well. It is time to realize that you are more powerful than your hurt.

Begin to set aside a daily time to breathe deeply, exhaling and inhaling slowly while focusing on letting go of your hurt. When you practice breathing techniques, you release all negative issues and people out of your mind and body.

That is why the first and last seven minutes of the day are so important. During those minutes you define what your day will be like. If you go to bed yelling and screaming or you wake up daily rushing, then your day will be full of continuous chaos and confusion.

Why not instead start your day with peace and relaxation. Start a daily affirmation list about your new beginning. For example, say, "I will release my past and create a better, brighter future without shame, blame, guilt and embarrassment regarding my past relationships."

Don't Blame Yourself

Women have a tendency to think we did everything wrong in the relationship. We begin to ask ourselves, "Why has another relationship gone bad?" or "What did I do wrong?" If this is you and you were involved with a version of THAT MAN discussed in the previous sections, know that was not all your fault; it may not be your fault at all. Those men were damaged, and they passed that damage on to you (including Daddy Damage). They are not good for anyone and are in need of professional help.

It could be that he was highly critical of you and said you were the blame for the breakup because you did not meet his standards. We as women have to stop accepting THAT MAN's blame, shame and guilt for the end of the relationship.

The truth is you may have done everything right and still ended up breaking up with THAT MAN. Remember, he is unhealthy, and it would never have worked unless the both of you were operating out of a healthy frame of mind.

Don't blame yourself if you were giving your all to the relationship. If you were committed to him and constantly made sacrifices for the benefit of the relationship, you were placing a high priority on making it work. This is what you are supposed to do, you just did it with the wrong type of man.

"What did I do wrong?" should not be your question. The question should be, "What did I do right and what did he do right and wrong in the relationship?" Ultimately, it is good to review your mistakes and know the warning signs so you can avoid repeating the same behaviors in the next relationship.

I have worked with many women over my twenty-two years in private practice, and I've found out that they tend to stay in relationships about three years too long.

The relationship is dead, but some women are too comfortable or too afraid to leave. Women come into my office and say, "I have not been in love with him for some time but I have to stay for the kids, for the money or (*fill in the blank*)."

You have to give up thinking you can change THAT MAN or believing that he will love you enough to do right by you. These beliefs are all based on the Daddy Damage taking over your mind and heart. You must trust the instincts that are telling you it is time to let go and move on.

Embarrassment

There is a time in every woman's life when she says, "What was I thinking?"; "Oh my God, I can't believe I was so stupid!"; or "I must have been crazy to have put up with that foolishness!"

Let's face it. We all have had experience with THAT MAN at one point or another. The morning after, or after the relationship ends, you hope you do not run into him in the mall, at the club, on the beach or in a board meeting. If you do see him, you turn your face, cross over to the other side of the room or try to avoid him at all costs. This is embarrassment, and it's something every human will face at some point in their life.

The word embarrassment means "to cause confusion and shame; to make incontestable self-conscious discomfort." It is the emotion that helps you to keep yourself in check.

When you have been with a man with whom you regret giving your time, energy, love and body, you feel embarrassed around him. I believe it is because now, after the fact, you realize how undeserving he was of you.

You realize that out of desperation, isolation, loneliness or fear of never finding the right man, you gave yourself to him. It is okay to be embarrassed. It is not okay to continue to stay with THAT MAN and to be made a fool over and over again. Let it go. Don't allow your past to dictate your present or future.

Someone once said to me, "With information comes education." Take this bit of information you are receiving today and educate yourself about how to know when to let a man into your life and when to walk away.

It is "time out" for us to keep repeatedly experiencing shame, blame and guilt over the mistakes of our past. Why? You cannot do anything about it except learn from the experience, and never, ever do it again. In case you didn't know, this is education that ultimately leads to wisdom in the next relationship.

Yes, it happened. But it's over and now you are wiser because of it. Embarrassment can only control you if you continue to think about yourself and allow yourself to become self-conscious about your actions whenever you see that person.

When you do this, you are allowing that person to have power over you and your present state of mind. Free yourself from your own self-victimization. Say with me, "I forgive myself for my past mistakes, and my future relationship will be much better than my past ones!"

Anger

Anger is a very powerful emotion. We all know of at least one woman who has keyed a car, broken out a window, put sugar in his tank or stayed outside of his house all night long waiting for him to return. You know someone who just went plum "off" on THAT MAN. You know a woman who has almost lost her mind over the wrong man.

When you are left alone with your thoughts, you can come up with some pretty devious ways to make THAT MAN pay for all the heartache you had to endure. You can be very spiteful and display very dangerous signs of anger. As a woman you are either very angry or you believe you have no right to display anger, because "nice girls don't get angry." When you get fed up, you say, "Enough is enough!" Then, THAT MAN who once made you laugh but now continually makes you cry had better watch out!

On the other side of this coin is the woman who won't allow herself to be angry. If this is you, it's time to embrace your anger and yell, scream, hit things, break things and release the pain you have experienced from being in a bad relationship. I have counseled numerous women who have told me, "It's not okay for me to show anger because: a) he will leave me; b) my family never showed anger so I don't know how to be angry; or c) intelligent women know how to control themselves and their anger.

I always find myself saying to these women, "Anger is a natural emotion, and it was given to us to help us process our pain and hurt. If you don't use it, it will remain bottled up inside of you and eventually turn into depression." This is the reason so many women are depressed, because they will not let out their anger when they need to. They operate in fear and continue to stay in a relationship that is slowly killing them.

If anger goes unexpressed for too long, it will come out eventually in an unhealthy way. When you have too much anger stored inside you and you don't release it, you can have what I call a volcanic eruption, and you become "Sister Supernova."

Who is a Sister Supernova? She is your alter ego, who acts in a way that ensures everyone around you pays for the pain THAT MAN caused you. When you are mean all the time, your girlfriends stop calling you to hang out with them because they don't want to deal with your negativity. The sad thing about this is, when they try to tell you about yourself, you don't listen and become even angrier at everyone but the one person who deserves the anger — THAT MAN!

Oh no! You would not dare show anger towards him. But, why's that? It's because he would then leave you. Look girlfriend, he was gone a long time ago, when he started to be THAT MAN. So stop making everyone else pay for his abuse and mistreatment of you. Give the anger to the person who deserves it and move on!

Revenge

Revenge is never a healthy way to deal with your pain. Initially, nearly every woman believes if she gets back at him, it will cause him to hurt too. But in actuality you just end up creating more hurt and pain for you to work through yourself.

I know you know, and all other women know, that when a woman seeks revenge she has had enough, and she is angry and hurting deeply. But we also know that she is not thinking clearly and therefore begins to act out in ways that are totally out of her character.

Some women seeking revenge will go out and flirt or even sleep with other men. Other women have been known to publicly humiliate THAT MAN, while others have been known to destroy his personal property. She may key his car, burn down the house, kill the dogs or even poison THAT MAN. I have counseled some women who have acted out in different ways and every one of them says after the fact, "It wasn't worth it." It wasn't worth the pain. It wasn't worth the court date or the jail time. It wasn't worth the debt they accumulated from having to pay to fix his car.

Some women don't act impulsively, but begin to plot ways to get him back. The thought of revenge is so good she sometimes even creates a plan. I tell my clients all the time, "Say it, write it down in a journal, but please don't do it." It's good to get the emotion out but it's not good to let that emotion cause your own destruction. What seems right to do at the moment only prolongs your pain. You end up having after-thoughts about what you did to yourself while thinking you were hurting him. Now you have to work through new thoughts, emotions and the results of your actions.

It's difficult for most women to handle these emotions and deal with the aftereffects of their behaviors, because women were built to love people and nurture them. So, when you go against your natural tendency, you are left feeling regret, remorse, and humiliation. The internal pain that you just caused yourself can take you years to work out of your soul.

As women we hold onto things in our soul's realm, and therefore take longer to release them. We are born to incubate. We incubate our children for nine months before they are born and once they come out our natural mothering instinct kicks in. We begin to sing, rock, and feed the baby. We love that baby. Nothing compares with the feelings that a woman has after becoming a mother.

You recall all the movement inside your belly and womb, the pain of labor when you gave birth and the love you felt once the baby was out and placed on your chest. These are all of the emotions that began from that soul attachment that was created while your baby was in the womb.

Those are the same emotions you experience when you have a relationship attachment with a man. Whether it is a healthy or unhealthy attachment, it doesn't matter. Your body still remembers the love, sadness, anger, hurt, silly times and fear.

Therefore, when you choose to seek out revenge on THAT MAN, the unhealthy emotions associated with the relationship are the emotions you are choosing to allow to control you. You are stronger and better than that, so don't allow your anger, sadness, or hurt to ruin your body and cause you to do unnecessary damage to yourself in the name of revenge.

Depression

This book would not be complete without a section on depression. Depression is that ugly monster that no woman wants to admit to having, but let's face it every woman has been depressed at some point in her life because of THAT MAN.

The question becomes, "Did you recover from it or is it still an ongoing part of your life?" First, let me make it perfectly clear that I am not referring to clinical depression that must be treated through medication. I am referring to depression you have brought upon yourself because you won't let THAT MAN go.

Make sure you allow yourself to see who this man TRULY is. He is the man who keeps making you feel good sexually but also makes Kim, Alicia and Shelia feel good too. He is the man who emptied out your bank account, went to Las Vegas with his boys and called you from a cell phone and said, "Yeah, I took it."

He is THAT MAN who told you he didn't want kids, but after five years you find out that he has fathered two children by two different women while he has been with you. He is the man who two days ago told you he would never hit you again, steal from you again, yell at you again, or use drugs or alcohol again, only to turn around and do all of those things, and more, again. You know THAT MAN!

But also know, he is the reason for your depression. No, you do not have a chemical imbalance. What you have is a self-esteem imbalance. You have allowed your worth to be tied up in THAT MAN. Stop crying, worrying, being scared to be alone, and simply leave THAT MAN alone. You can do it.

Yes, it is going to hurt, and yes, you are going to be sad and you will cry. You may even have some sleepless nights, times you won't want to eat; and you will have diarrhea, nausea, feel stupid, and not be able to focus at work or at home.

When you drive home, you may go through stoplights and stop signs. You may get home, park your car, put your key into your door, take off your clothes and not remember how you got into your bed. Then you will begin to cry and feel horrible inside.

You may feel like you just got run over by a Mack truck. You will not want to get out of bed and you may even call off work the next day. This cycle will repeat itself until you are totally over THAT MAN.

Understand that what you are experiencing is your normal grief cycle. You have to grieve so you won't become depressed. If you do not allow yourself to grieve you will eventually go into a deeper state of depression.

Once you begin to let go, please do not go back. If you return to the relationship, it makes it that much harder to leave again. That's because when you return sometimes the connection you feel to him seems even stronger.

No one likes to be emotionally, physically and mentally ill. But to get over THAT MAN, you have to experience all three of these states. There is no way around this healing cycle. So, let yourself cry, be ill, have some sleepless nights and think over what went wrong in the relationship. Just don't go back.

Remember, there is a reason or two or three that you left him in the first place. If you need to, write all the reasons down again as a reminder.

Shame

We have all done something that brings shame. Remember when you were a kid and you brought shame upon yourself? Or maybe you were an adult when it happened and you thought about what your parents would think if they found out.?

Shame makes you feel small, dishonored, regretful and disgraced. When a woman has dealt with THAT MAN, sometimes these emotions are a part of her everyday experiences.

Different women I have worked with over the years have told me about various perverted sexual acts they did to keep THAT MAN. Other women have told me about lies they have told to THAT MAN's boss or his mother to hold on to him and the relationship.

You are experiencing shame any time you feel uncomfortable doing something, and it makes you feel regret, ridiculous or your conscience says, "What are you doing?" From a clinical point of view, shame is when you have the same feeling as if you were standing in front of your mom, and she is shaking her finger back and forth at you saying, "No, no, no! You know I raised you better than that!"

Being with THAT MAN can cause a whole lot of shame in a great woman. During the course of your relationship with THAT MAN, you somewhere stopped defining for yourself what is good for you. As a woman you have a right to say, "This is my body and I will not allow you to abuse it."

As a woman you have a right to say, "No, I will not lie to your mother. I will not have a "ménage a trois" (three-person sexual encounter). I will not cosign for you to buy a car."

To let go of your shame, you must stop doing those things that go against your moral and spiritual values and beliefs. Make a vow to yourself to only do those things that bring honor and respect to you and your womanhood.

Today, become your own accountability partner and make a pledge to yourself to no longer do things that will bring shame on you, whether it's for THAT MAN or for anyone else.

Guilt

When discussing guilt with people from a clinical perspective, we let them know that guilt is to be felt and experienced when you intentionally set out to hurt or harm someone. It's not when someone has intentionally or unintentionally hurt you.

If THAT MAN intentionally or unintentionally hurt you by lying, stealing, cheating, being a "down-low" brother or by just treating you poorly, you do not have a reason to hold onto guilt.

Why do you feel guilty? You did nothing wrong. You did not create a plan to hurt THAT MAN or anyone in his family.

If you had said, "Yeah, I'll show him, I'll get him back," and you created a plan and carried it out, that's a different story. Then you have a reason to be guilty. However, most women go around feeling guilty about situations and things that happened inside their relationship that were not their fault and totally out of their control.

If you have been experiencing guilt over some things that happened with you and THAT MAN, and you have been continually punishing yourself for it, stop! Release it! It's not your guilt to carry.

Ask yourself, "Did I intentionally set out to hurt or harm him? Was what happened premeditated on my part?" If the answer to these questions is "no," then stop letting guilt control you. Say to yourself, "I did nothing wrong, so I have no reason to feel guilty! He did all that stuff to me! He lied, he cheated, and he messed up the money and he hit me! I will not go on experiencing guilt over THAT MAN!"

Now say that over and over again to yourself until you begin to believe it. The more you speak something aloud, the more power you give to those words. Repetition is the key to bringing forth life and power in your words. So you need to begin speaking your new affirmation to help you overcome your guilt regarding THAT MAN right now.

Self Esteen/Worth

Self-esteem comes out of confidence and satisfaction in oneself. When a woman has been with THAT MAN for a long time, he can and ultimately does damage her self-esteem.

When a woman begins to question herself all the time, her self-esteem has been damaged. If you are a woman who says, "I hate my body, my skin color, my job, et cetera" because THAT MAN constantly puts you down, you have now developed self-esteem issues. If these issues were non-existent before you met him, then he is the cause of it all.

What has happened is that you have bought into the lies he has told you over the time you two were together. You allowed them to set up shop in your mind, and they have lodged in your soul. Now it is time for you to get them out.

The first step to regaining your confidence and self-esteem is to create ten affirmations you will say daily. For example, I say, "I am worthy of love and respect." and "I am wise. I will not accept anyone's shame, guilt or lies."

You have to be your first and best cheerleader every day. If you don't tell yourself you are beautiful, why would you expect other people to tell you that you are? Your self-esteem comes from within. You develop it or you destroy it. It's your choice.

The next thing you need to do is to tear up all the negative mind tapes you have been playing over and over again from THAT MAN! Write them all down, then write down the opposite of what he told you about yourself. If he said "You are fat and flat-chested," you say, "I am full-figured and I have great breasts!"

Whatever he said to try to destroy your self-esteem, you write out the exact opposite of what he said to strengthen your self-esteem. Remember, your self-esteem is the positive statement you say to yourself over and over again, which brings good thoughts, emotions, and attracts good people into your life.

Finally, keep your self-esteem elevated by looking at yourself daily in the mirror and praising everything about yourself. The best way to begin is to praise your physical self, then your mental, sexual, financial, and spiritual self. Create a list of daily confessions about all those areas of your life and watch how you begin to empower yourself. Also, watch your self-esteem and confidence improve.

Yes, you loved THAT MAN hard with all of your mind, body, and soul. You even took him back again and again and again, but now you are no longer allowing THAT MAN to trick you into giving him one more try. There will be no more of the foolish games he played, the crazy lies he told, the numerous letdowns. They are all over now and you can go on with your life. Tell yourself, "Today I will begin a new life with more love, power, and honor for myself than ever before."

Man-Sharing

What is "man-sharing," you ask? This is when a woman goes out with, sleeps with, or entertains any man that she knows belongs to another woman. As mentioned earlier in this book, I am speaking to those women who are adulterers, mistresses, side pieces, and jump-offs — anyone who knows they are spending time with another woman's man and just don't care.

This woman has some personal issues. Due to previous damage from past relationships, she has lost respect for herself. She may be lonely. She has negative self-esteem, and because of past hurt and trauma she now tries to protect her heart by man-sharing.

If you are that woman, I hope reading this will help you to stop it! Man-sharing can only be done if we women allow it. Men can't do anything to us unless we give them approval and too many women are saying this behavior is okay.

When you disrespect other women by sleeping with, talking to, cooking for, or giving money to their men, you are allowing yourself to be played. THAT MAN always goes home to her, never to you!

You will always be number two, never number one. This is a horrible way to live, and please don't try to justify your behavior by saying, "Well, I don't want a man. I don't have to deal with all of his bad behaviors. I get the fun, good side." That is a lie you tell yourself to help you be okay with how you are disrespecting yourself. Respect is simply treating others how you want to be treated. If you are not respecting other women, don't expect them to respect you. So when the man you love steps out on you with a side piece, don't say, "How could you?", because you have been that side piece to someone else.

I am a true believer in reaping and sowing, or karma, as some of my clients call it. So ladies, if you don't want this to happen to you in your relationship, please don't do it to another woman. Respect yourself.

As mentioned, women who man-share usually have negative or no self-esteem. These women have been damaged, broken, and mistreated in personal and intimate relationships, and now all they want to do is feel better. Feeling better never comes, because they continue to repeat their cycle of pain by entering into unhealthy relationships with men who will never be available to commit to them.

Women who man-share usually have Daddy Damage, mommy mis-handling, and boyfriend blues stories. These are all relationships in which healthy attachments were never established. Now the women go from one unavailable man to another to avoid healthy relationships for fear of being hurt. This in turn causes the woman to hurt other women and repeatedly hurt herself.

To be a healthy woman you can't entertain another woman's man, ever! I don't want to hear this anymore: "Well, another woman did it to me! Who cares about her?" So you want to be broken and damaged goods like her? Wow! Really? Stop your whining and crying and begin to say, "I feel sorry for her."

If you choose to take that road (the revenge road), just know you will start a vicious cycle upon yourself and you will begin a pattern of sowing and reaping terrible things into your life. Being mentally healthy means not doing something that may make you feel good emotionally or sexually for the moment, but later having lifelong regrets about it.

Your self-esteem is not wrapped up in a man or relationship. Your self-esteem comes from inside you. You control whether your self-esteem will be negative or positive, not anyone else.

Those people who hurt you and caused you pain are no longer with you. Becoming like them doesn't hurt them, only you. As women, we have to stop saying and acting on the mindset of, "Now I'm going to get them back" or "It's my turn to get what I want," not realizing that you again are making deposits into your soul that you will carry around with you for some time. We only set ourselves up for more damage. A woman who shares men needs therapy so she can get to the core of why she does this and what she can do to learn to overcome these negative behaviors.

If you are a woman who is feeling lonely, don't say, "A piece of a man is better than no man at all." That is just another lie a woman tells herself to justify being with someone else's man. A woman who cannot enjoy time by herself without a man is also broken. There isn't a reason to have a man all of the time, and to feel if you don't have a man you are not complete. There are more women in the world than men, so let's face it: at some point some women are not going to have a man. It's up to us as women to become comfortable with this.

It is better to have loved and lost than to never have loved at all. I once heard someone say. Imagine, if you had never experienced a man's touch or a healthy relationship. I believe most women reading this book have experienced those things at some point. In the next relationship you just want him to treat you right.

It is *okay* for a woman to go to dinner, a club, or a movie alone. Until you start enjoying your time alone with yourself, you will not be able to be okay without a man. For some women, the best times in their lives have been when they have been without a man. Why? It's because the headaches, heartaches, highs and lows of a relationship are nonexistent. When you are by yourself, there is a freedom in being able to go where you want to go, when you want to go, and not having to check in with anyone about finances, children, trips, going out with friends, spending time with your parents, whew! Need I say more?

Women, many times we want what we don't have and don't appreciate what we do have. Learn how to appreciate yourself. Don't look for THAT MAN to show you appreciation anymore, especially if he belongs to someone else. Enjoy yourself! Some of my best moments were and are when I am alone. I enjoy people-watching at a restaurant and I enjoy a good movie by myself. These are the best times for me to think about my wants, my dreams and the areas I need to improve on.

Being alone can be a great thing if you learn to use that time for reflection and introspection. Peace with yourself and joy about what you are doing right in your life is comparable to nothing! Therefore, know and understand that the more time you spend with you alone, the better you will begin to feel about yourself. You'll realize that being alone with yourself, in reality, isn't all that bad.

Lack of Trust

Lack of trust is an issue most people struggle with after experiencing a heart wound. Relationship recovery is one of the deepest heart wounds around. When you give someone your trust you say to them, "Here are my life, my heart, my soul, and my body. Take it and protect it at all times." You trust that the person you have given your all to will do their best to protect the one thing you value most: yourself.

A man can be faithful to one woman if he so chooses. But there are men who choose to have no morals, and every woman is his for the taking. These men are the ones women are recovering from in this book. As a relationship grows you begin to trust the man on a deeper level and a deeper level of commitment develops as time goes on. This trust and commitment cause you to believe THAT MAN would never break your trust because he values you and your happiness. So, when you find out he has betrayed you, you are devastated, disgusted and heartbroken.

The relationship grief cycle begins. When you find out the man has cheated, the shock, denial, sadness, anger, anguish, hurt and fear begins. A woman goes through all of these emotions before healing is truly complete.

There are several types of deep betrayal. The first one, which I call Type One betrayal, takes place when your man cheats on you with a woman you do not know. This could be a woman he met on a trip, works with, or someone he just met out in the community. She may know nothing about you, or, as mentioned, she may know and simply not care.

In Type One betrayal there are psychological symptoms that manifest for women, which are very similar to the grief cycle.

You may play private eye and begin to go through your man's car, clothes and wallet. You might also follow him to work, trail him around the city and check in his car, or hire a real private investigator to do it for you. You may even have your girlfriend call him and act like someone who wants to "hook up with him." This is the relationship paranoia that is created by the betrayal of trust.

Women come into the office all the time and say, "I am not myself. I have never checked the phone bill, gone through his pockets or looked through his cell phone." When someone you love destroys your trust you sink into stalking mode. You begin to do things totally out of character and you begin to hate the woman in the mirror. This betrayal causes you to become someone you don't even recognize.

Relationship paranoia also leads to the "other woman" being called on the telephone, confronted in person by the wife or girlfriend, or even being beaten up by other women. And, if the other woman didn't know the girlfriend or wife existed this is devastating for both of them, because he didn't place the same value on the relationship as the women did.

In this case, whether you are the main woman or the other woman, your wound further deepens as you realize the moral, emotional and physical bond you thought existed between you and THAT MAN was a lie. Now the relationship depressive may take you days or months to get to a place of acceptance, meaning you realize all that happened wasn't your fault and you are a morally just person.

Type Two betrayal is betrayal by your man and one of your close female friends; she may have even been your best friend. Where Type One betrayal may last days or months, Type Two betrayals may last years. This emotional wound goes so deep because not only are you dealing with the knowledge that your best friend slept with your man, you are also dealing with the loss of a friendship as well.

You expect your best friend to never sleep with your man, tell your deepest darkest secrets, or talk behind your back to another girlfriend. In other words, you never expect her to break your trust. Of course, you never expect your boyfriend or lover to do that to you either, and it's even more devastating when he's your husband.

When your trust is broken by two people you love dearly at the same time, it is a double whammy! You feel like your world has imploded on you. You are built to be long-suffering, patient and trusting, but when someone breaks your trust, you find it hard to release the hurt and move forward. This is part of your "holding onto things" as well. Trust once broken is hard to regain; therefore, when you are betrayed by your man and your best friend, you experience depression in the worst way.

The most difficult woman to treat in therapy is the woman whose man cheated, and ultimately left her for, her best friend. She has to work through the relationship grief cycle process, rage, rejection and the heart-wrenching wounds of the loss of two very important people in her life.

Most women take a long time to establish friends that they refer to as "best friends." These may be women in their lives from childhood. So, when a lifelong friend is lost due to betrayal, the hurting woman must work through all of the years that are lost from that friendship as well as the betrayal by THAT MAN. Sometimes you may question the friend's loyalty in other areas as well, because now your mind plays tricks on you. You think, "Was she ever really trustworthy at all?" You begin to think about secrets you shared, trips you took and talks you had; advice given; and conversations you had about THAT MAN.

You begin to evaluate everything you ever told the ex-friend about your relationship with THAT MAN and any other man. Then you wonder if you had any responsibility for them cheating together. This self-questioning and self-doubt ultimately lead to you isolating yourself from other women, saying, "I do not trust women." or "I can't get along with women." We've all heard a woman say, "I get along better with men or all of my best friends are men." You have male best friends because some woman in your past hurt you deeply and therefore you decided not to trust another woman ever again, because the pain was so deep and the wound never healed.

When your best friend and your man cheat, the emotions you experience are equivalent that of losing two parents in an airplane crash at the same time. When we lose those we love suddenly, our mind and body goes into a state of shock.

We go from having those people actively in our lives on a daily basis to no contact at all. This is a traumatic incident and there needs to be a time of shutting down to process the emotions and psychological pain that goes along with a Type Two betrayal. If you're going through this time of issue, it would be wise to seek professional help for a period of six to nine months, just to be able to manage life without thinking you are losing your mind.

Type Two betrayals are difficult to recover from, but it can be done. You will most likely be afraid of dating, and of trusting other women again for quite some time. One of the goals in this recovery process is to recognize that not every man cheats, and that only the woman to be angry with is the one who cheated with your man, not the entire female gender. Another goal is to not get stuck in a place of pain that punishes people. If you get stuck, you may miss out on a lot of healthy relationships because of one unhealthy wicked woman and lousy man.

Remember, we all have made mistakes and need to receive forgiveness at some time in our lives. If you are hurting, your goal is to overcome your pain and ultimately FORGIVE those two people who hurt you so deeply. You will trust and love again, but first you must forgive.

Resentment

Women are not built to hold onto anger or to be unforgiving toward others. Forgiveness happens when we set the person who has harmed us free from our anger. We forgive them of all their wrongdoing, just like at one point in time someone did for us.

The woman you are doesn't allow for you to hold onto unforgiveness toward THAT MAN and dare to call yourself whole and healthy. Being whole and being healthy means having forgiveness for those whom we think don't deserve it.

If you hold onto your unforgiveness towards that person, you will only end up going down one of two roads — the road of bitterness or the road of resentment.

The bitterness road leaves you feeling severe pain and you become very cynical. Resentment is a feeling of pain and hatred directed at someone you feel wronged you in some way. The resentment road makes you become repeatedly indignant and repeatedly show ill will to the person, because you feel justified.

You may find yourself always badmouthing men and putting all males into the same category. This is unfair. Not all men hurt you, just THAT MAN. Therefore, THAT MAN is the only male who deserves all of your anger, hurt, unforgiveness and resentment, that is, if you choose to stay stuck in an unhealthy emotional state.

When you are bitter, you cannot find anything good to say and you use a lot of cynicism to help you feel better. You distrust men and their motives, so you begin to treat them like THAT MAN Man treated you.

You might start to date a nice guy but because THAT MAN did whatever he did to you, you now have trust issues. You are cynical, bitter and think this new guy will do the same thing to you because you believe he is operating out of the same selfish motives as THAT MAN. This usually is not true, and this is how a woman will sabotage her new relationship because she has not worked through her unforgiveness of That Man. The new gentleman says, "Forget it. I can't take your attitude and negative behavior towards me any longer." If you keep up your negative attitude you will continue to lose good men.

The other road is resentment. Resentment is different from bitterness in that you show your anger towards this person who actually hurt you time and time again. The problem with this is THAT MAN has moved on, so in holding onto resentment you are only hurting yourself.

I once worked with a woman who had been divorced from her husband for several years. She was now married to someone else and claimed to be happy. The problem was that her husband felt she was always mean to her ex-husband when he came to pick up the children.

She often would say mean things to him about their past and everything he had done wrong in their marriage. She told me she believed he needed to hear it over and over again so he never did this to another woman.

Her current husband told me that her ex had said he was sorry on numerous occasions, that he was a fool to have done what he did and now he was a changed man. The woman's current husband even said he liked her ex-husband and that they got along fine. Yet the woman's resentment was causing her to stay stuck in her past and impacting her new marriage in a negative way. She was not only resentful but bitter as well, often treating her current husband the same way by making critical and cynical comments.

She even compared him to her ex, which was probably the worst insult she could have given him.

Forgiveness

As the above example shows, when you choose to withhold forgiveness you get stuck in one of the healing cycles and can't get out. An event may have happened ten years ago and yet you still think about it like it was yesterday. People you tell the story to are shocked when they find out it occurred so far in the past because your intensity and use of the present tense makes them assume the event was recent.

Another result of un-forgiveness is difficulty with other relationships. In my practice I have heard all too often. "Men can't be trusted," or "I was hurt by a woman before and now I only have male friends."

These are ways of keeping your walls of protection high and avoiding the deeper issues at hand: your lack of forgiveness! You must allow yourself to trust again. *All women are not untrustworthy, nor are all men.*

Singer, songwriter and actress Jill Scott once said, "Love has left me cold....God, I need your healing." You too must allow the wounds to be healed properly, and this may mean taking more risks with women friends and allowing yourself to be open to the possibility of a new trustworthy woman friend walking into your life. Men can be trustworthy too. It goes back to allowing your secondary attraction characteristics to be the primary force operating in your dating cycle, not your primary attraction characteristics. More about that in the next section.

Once forgiveness is reached, acceptance is the next task of healing.

Acceptance simply means having an understanding of the reality of a situation (including its negative effects on you) and being okay with the fact that you cannot go back in time and undo it.

When you accept that this is a part of your growth process, you are able to put this incident in its proper chapter of your life. No one told us we would have relationships free of heartache. Different trials and struggles in our lives only push us forward and cause us to become more mentally and emotionally strong.

Part Three
Life Is Grand Again: Preparing For The Next Relationship

Life Is Grand Again Relationship Recovery Techniques

It was New Year's Day and my family and I were returning home from a trip to Miami. Earlier, as we sat in a restaurant, we couldn't help overhearing the loud conversation of three single women nearby speaking about the past year and the men they had dated.

I found it funny that each of them stated, "It's the New Year and I am going to find the right man." I guess I have always had a little issue with women being on the prowl and trying to find the "right man." Historically men found the women. Even the Bible says, "He who finds a wife finds a good thing."

I think sometimes this is where women go wrong. I believe it's okay to be assertive, to ask a man to dance, to approach a man; however, I think we need to draw the line when it comes to asking him to marry us or giving too many ultimatums, being controlling or taking charge too much. Numerous men have told me that when women propose or pressure them to marry them, they believe the woman will want to control the relationship in the future. In some situations this may not be the case at all, yet before taking this step it makes sense to consider your man, his personality, and how he engages with you. Based on what you know about your man, would he be offended if you requested that he propose to you, or if you proposed to him?

I have counseled many men, and every one of them repeatedly told me, "I can't stand a woman who is too aggressive, controlling and independent." Ladies, I don't care how much he tells you it is attractive to him. He is simply lying to you. These men continually come to me for therapy because, as the man says, "My wife or girlfriend really does not need a man."

In this chapter, I would like to give you some relationship techniques that will allow you to recover from the old relationship and have open eyes and ears to better prepare for the next man. Then we know life will be grand after THAT MAN.

Over my twenty years of counseling women and men about relationship issues, I have identified five key concepts we need to grasp to become ready for a healthy relationship and to identify the relationship patterns that have us repeating the same mistakes, over and over.

Primary Attraction Characteristics

Everyone has a type of person that he or she is attracted to naturally — this is what some people call "animal attraction." As humans, we have hormones that cause us to look at other people and, based on what we see, say, "Oh, he is fine!" or "OMG, he is so ugly!"

Well, it's time to figure out what goes into your primary attraction characteristics.

The primary attraction characteristics are those enacted through the use of our senses. So, when you initially see a man, what you see, hear, smell, touch and taste are heightened. If I were to rank order a woman's senses it would be sight, sound, smell, taste and then touch.

I rank these in this order because nearly every woman I have ever spoken with has told me that sight is her primary attraction sense. We are easily swayed by our primary attraction characteristics. They often get women into trouble because they are based on surface attributes, not characteristics that support a relationship over time.

Our senses, which guide our body, are also connected to our soul. Women also get into trouble when they allow the senses to control how they operate in a relationship. I will expound on each sense, to give a better understanding of how primary attraction characteristics work.

Sight: We have heard the saying, "The eyes are the window to the soul." That may be, but through our eyes we also receive all types of information and make judgments about it, for example, whether it is aesthetically pleasing or not. If through our eye gate we decide, yes, something is beautiful, we then mentally check off that it is okay to move on to our next sense.

We all know if a guy who does not fit your view of what is aesthetically appealing walks up to you, you will quickly look away. Let's say two men approach you on the same evening, One is over six feet tall, with nice skin and an athletic build, smells wonderful, and has beautiful deep dimples and a smile. He also has on the perfect outfit that allows you to catch a glimpse of his pectoral muscles.

The other gentleman also has nice skin, smells wonderful and has beautiful, deep dimples and dresses nice. But he is five-foot, six inches tall and has a potbelly. Who are you initially attracted to? Who would be your secondary attraction guy? What are your preconceived notions about each man and why?

What if I told you that the man you were initially attracted to was unemployed, lives with his mother and has five children by three different women, and the gentleman you were not attracted to was a millionaire? Would that make a difference as to who is more attractive to you? If you choose based on looks alone, you will miss out on the wealthy gentleman.

If you see a gentleman and he doesn't look at least ninety to ninety-five percent of what you want you look past him and perhaps past some good opportunities. Now I'm not saying you have to marry him, but men are like gifts to women. Some are beautifully wrapped, but when you open them, they are truly not what you wanted. You don't know what kind of gift you are getting if you only stare at the wrapping and never open the package.

If you decide to date a guy based on his looks, then you are only dealing with the wrapping and not the real gift. A smart woman would give both of the gentlemen at least one date before she makes a decision as to whether he fits her profile.

Sound: I could say a lot about our ears, and how we've allowed what men have said to mislead us into believing he's the man for us. What women have heard has led to pain, trust and insecurity issues. As mentioned earlier, sometimes the first man to lie to us was our father, and this just created a wound in us that continued to grow with every man that came into our lives after that.

You go into a relationship with great expectations. And when THAT MAN begins to tell you what he will do for you and how he loves you, you just fall deeper and deeper into a place of connection with him.

Women want to hear how a man will provide for and protect them. Our ears allow us to hear those things that make us happy, sad, angry, scared or secure.

We all want to hear the good and not the bad. Hearing, be it a voice or other kind of sound, has a way of sending certain emotions through us, causing us to quiver, shake and feel all mushy inside.

It makes me think back to when I attended a concert in Atlanta, where a male singer was performing and I watched numerous women take their panties to him up on stage. These women did all this based on the words he was singing. The sound of a man's voice can be so deep, so strong, so powerful.

Many women have gotten into trouble at some point because some man said the right thing at the right time and, as one of my clients said, "My panties just fell off."

The words we hear are so powerful they can make us laugh or they can make us cry. The words we hear can destroy our self-worth or make it soar. We know the difference in a man's voice when he is pleased with us, and we also know when THAT MAN is unhappy with us.

When you learn to listen to the sound of a man's voice, you identify the pitch and tones that make you feel different emotions when he is speaking to you. Learn to respect your "ear gate." There are men in the world who have trained their voices to cause you to respond in a certain way, to cause you to "throw your panties on the stage," so to speak. As a woman, you need to become aware of what he said that caused you to melt.

Smell: About six months ago my husband bought this cologne while we were on vacation. The first time he put it on everything inside of me started to quiver. It smelled so good that I instantly wanted to attack him! I was excited and very attracted to him, just from the smell of that cologne. I had not smelled cologne that ignited my hormones in a long time.

Smell is powerful. The right smell on a man can make your heart palpitate, your eyes roll back in your head and your body go limp in his arms. For some women, the sense of smell is the most distinctive one. Webster's Dictionary defines it as "to perceive something by its odor or scent." When a man smells good, it just does something to you and when a man smells horrible that also does something to you. Also, some women are attracted to men who smell rugged, sweaty or like the great outdoors.

Every woman should know the top three scents she enjoys on a man and how they arouse her; she should also learn how to control her responses to these scents. If you can't differentiate between your primary smell attraction and the arousal it causes in you, you may end up dating a few men you should have left alone.

If a man approaches you and he is aesthetically pleasing, his voice is wonderfully sexy and he smells good, it just may be over for you before anything really begins, because you are overtaken by your primary attraction characteristics.

The next time a man's sense has you going "oooh, ahh" or "Oh my goodness, what is that terrible smell?" take a moment to ask yourself what you need to know about him before you make a decision to go out or sleep with him, or pass him by. It just may stop you from doing something you later regret.

Taste: When I think about taste, I am reminded of the movie "Pretty Woman" and how Julia Roberts said, "I don't ever kiss a guy on the mouth; it's too personal." That was a powerful statement that she was making and a lot of people, I believe, missed it.

As human beings, once we taste something it remains in our memory banks. Many people can recall the first sweet-tasting item they experienced as well as the worst thing they have tasted. When you think of this in terms of tasting a man's lips, it can become dangerous.

When you taste something, you are getting all kinds of flavor from it. And, when you are kissing a man you are getting all kinds of flavor from him. Ever think about why most people never forget their first kiss? You remember his name and where you were, what you were wearing, what grade you were in and the way he kissed you. If your memory is really good, you can recall how long the kiss lasted.

A kiss is contact (touch), flavor, emotion and intimacy, all in one. We will discuss contact in the next section. As for flavor, when you taste a man through a tongue kiss it sends an erotic sensation through your whole body. The pleasure zones become heightened and there is a chemical release that makes you desire him more, especially if he is a good kisser. On the other hand, a bad kiss can send you running.

I have worked with women who said to me, "He wanted to taste my lips" or "He wanted to taste my tongue." These women are captured by the man's ability to send those erotic sensations through her body just by the kiss.

Women have said things like, "He used a peppermint on his tongue and transferred it to mine or he played around in my mouth with his tongue and this really excited me. Most of them had never experienced any type of oral (mouth) foreplay. Therefore, this type of "tasting" caused the women to fall for THAT MAN.

It is important to remember that primary attraction usually gets you into trouble. This is because as women we are very aroused by our senses, and we hold every experience in our soul. We often recall events that men forget, and we have sensations that go with them.

Exercise: My First Kiss

Right now, close your eyes and recall your first REAL kiss. This is the kiss that got you aroused and feeling warm inside. Where were you standing? What were you wearing? What about this memory is present with you right now? Now think about the guy. Was he your first love? A crush? Did he define the ways in which you like to be kissed? And just how did he kiss you? Now write that down and, moving forward, try not to let every guy you date kiss you in that way. Just like lovemaking is not for every guy you date, kissing deeply and intimately isn't either.

Limiting the number of men you allow to experience you through taste is important. You must have a standard that you go by and don't waver from it. It is acceptable to peck a guy on the cheek or on the lips, but to tongue kiss him on the first, second, or even third date may be putting yourself and your heart into serious jeopardy.

Touch: When I think about the power of touch, I am reminded of the birth of my first son. I remember the doctor taking my son, bathing him, then immediately placing my baby on my chest. She said, "Your baby needs to know your scent. The fastest way for him to connect to you is through skin-to-skin contact."

That was such a powerful statement to me. I knew then that when I nursed my son I was going to make sure we always had skin-to-skin contact because I wanted him to have a healthy attachment to his mother.

This same principle applies to a relationship between a man and a woman. Touch is so important when it comes to bonding and connectivity. To touch someone is to come into contact with and feel that person. When a man and woman touch, you are feeling that person on a deeper more intimate level.

For example, think about the last time you got into a fight with your boyfriend. When he wanted to touch you, if you were still upset, you jerked away. Most people, when they are angry, will not want the person they are angry with to touch them.

On the other hand, when you are happy with your man you will allow him to touch you all day long. Why? Touch causes you to feel good inside. It releases chemicals in the brain that tell you to be happy, smile, relax, and enjoy the emotion. That is the power of touch. It is so powerful that after lying skin to skin with your male for a while your hearts will begin to beat to the same rhythm.

When two people are making love they are truly one body; there is nothing that can come between them in that moment of intimacy. Because he is inside of you, you are connected, attached, literally "one being." The woman is experiencing THAT MAN in his entirety and vice versa. This is not something to be taken lightly.

When touch is happening, there are all kinds of deposits, mental and emotional, being made into you. The man is the depositor who sends the recurrent, and you are the receiver, who holds it. Because of this, you hold onto every guy who ever enters you.

That's why it is so hard to leave THAT MAN alone. He has connected with you and made deposits of love, trust, forgiveness and fear inside of you, and breaking that connection seems unthinkable.

Exercise: Recalling Soul Ties

Touching someone is very personal and intimate and, as seen in the example with my newborn son, it's a great way to connect to someone quickly. Or, think about when you're on a plane and the stranger next touches your arm by accident. You instinctively move away because this person just crossed an unspoken rule: "Don't touch me unless I say you can." Ask yourself, "Who am I connected to and who do I need to be disconnected from?" Make a list of the gentlemen in your life you allowed to touch you and penetrate you. Start first with the person you allowed to take your virginity. Isn't it amazing that we never forget the person? That is because our soul is strongly connected to him. He made the biggest deposit in our squish realm and every one of our five senses. Next, write down what types of things (good and bad habits) you picked up from them. Then begin to work to rid yourself of those things that have hindered you in other relationships.

Secondary Attraction Characteristics

Now that we have discussed the primary attraction characteristics, it's time to move on to secondary attraction characteristics — those you noticed after looking past the initial physical attraction. These are the traits of a man who is able to commit to you in a relationship, and those that will help you to stay committed as well.

I have found there are five characteristics that your man needs to have for that relationship to be able to withstand some damage. Now, all relationships experience damage; however, if you first put together a profile of the ideal man, your experiences with men who are incompatible will be far fewer. There are characteristics that women discuss in our counseling sessions that I believe are important: spirituality, finances, mother-son relationship; children, and mental stability.

Spirituality

First, it's important to have the same religious beliefs as your boyfriend. As I've seen time and time again in session, if he asks you to change your religious beliefs to be with him or vice versa, you eventually end up resenting each other and the relationship ends.

It is really hard to change your core beliefs and values for someone else. Those types of changes only come from within, not because of an ultimatum. In fact, I have seen that when a woman tries to become something she is not it ultimately leads to a state of depression, anxiety, or even bipolar disorder.

Think about the person or people (probably your parents, grandparents, or other guardian) who introduced you to your religion of choice. What was it about them or about the religion that made you believe in it? Was it their lifestyle? Was it the way they interacted with you? Was it what you saw and read for yourself?

Whatever the reason, those thoughts, values and beliefs are deeply ingrained in you, so if you were to change them as an adult it must be for reasons similar to those you experienced as a child. It should be because you decided on your own to change, not because of THAT MAN.

Finances

One day a woman walked into my office and said, "Oh my God, he had me marry him, buy a house with him and later I found out he had a kid and didn't pay his child support. Now they are taking money from my check to cover his child support."

When I began to ask her questions like, "Did you ask him if he had kids? Did you ask if he had any outstanding debt? Did you do a background check on him?" she started shaking her head. Her answer to all of these questions was no.

It is sad that you have to do some of these things, but the truth is all people have the capacity to lie and deny things in their lives. The point of dating is to get all the information you can about that person to help you make a well-informed decision about what type of future you may have together. Don't waste this valuable time because you are afraid to ask the hard questions.

In today's world, when you date someone you have to know his or her financial status. This is important because it allows you to go into the relationship with your eyes open about any financial hurdles to overcome. Some couples even decide that each person will take responsibility for paying off the debt they brought to the relationship. Everyone deals with their financial situation differently, but you cannot deal with it if you don't have all the facts.

Mother-Son Relationship

We've all heard the saying, "Watch how a man treats his mother and you will know how he will treat you." This statement is very true.

Many women I have counseled say things like, "He cusses his mother out. He has hit his mom." Others say, "If his mom calls, he will drop everything for her" or "His mother still tells him what to do in his life."

There are three types of "momma's boys" in the world: (a) The ones who do any and everything for their mothers; (b) The ones who can't stand their mothers; and (c) the ones who have healthy relationships with their mothers.

The first momma's boy has not yet separated from his mother. They are enmeshed, meaning she still has a great deal of control over his life. In some cases, this control is enough to destroy his relationships with women. When you're dating or married to THAT MAN, he runs at the drop of a dime when she calls, while you find yourself playing second fiddle.

These men may even be financing their mother's lifestyle. They are the ones who say, "My mom told me to become a lawyer but I really wanted to be an actor," or "My mom said that I shouldn't date you anymore because you are too needy." He then breaks up with you after a year of what you thought was a good relationship.

The second type of man is verbally, emotionally or even physically abusive to his mother. He may be seen cursing his mother out, pushing or hitting her, or even stealing money from her right in front of you. Know this: if he doesn't respect the woman who gave him life, you can't expect him to respect you.

A man who makes his mother cry and is abusive to her is really not a man at all. You have to be aware of the important message he is sending you here! Apparently he has a wound from his mother that hasn't been worked out and therefore, he cannot connect with any woman because he never connected with her. He needs therapy to help him overcome his heart wound.

Men who are abusive to their mothers have an attachment issue; therefore, THAT MAN can't give to you the closeness, intimacy, and love you need because he never received it from his own mother. The lack of connection with his mother created damage in him, and he passes that damage to the women he dates. This is not your fault, so don't allow him to abuse you or allow yourself to believe you did something to deserve this abusive behavior.

Finally, we have the male who has successfully developed a healthy, loving, balanced relationship with his mother. He loves her wisdom, values her spirit, and respects her as a person; you know this because he speaks of his mother in glowing terms. Yet he also has healthy boundaries with his mother and does not allow her to dictate who he dates, what he does for a living, or his friends. This man will be the type of man who can say no to his mother and not feel guilty about it. But he will also go to her aid in times of need.

He will also ask for your permission or input on situations involving his mother. And, the majority of the time, he will choose you over his mother to spend time with. This is a man with good parental boundaries, and the type you want in your life.

Mental Stability

Imagine a woman who dated a gentleman in college people often said was odd. For example, there were days when his coworkers would arrive at the job to find him writing weird poetry and making statements that seemed "off." The thing was, he was a straight-A student and never bothered anyone. Well, this woman went on to marry this man and ten years later he was diagnosed with schizophrenia and depression. By this time she had lived through years of unnecessary abusive behavior mentally, emotionally and verbally. The warning signs were there in college, but she just denied what she was hearing and seeing because she loved him.

One thing I have learned over my years counseling men is that they try everything in the world to hide their mental instability from those they love. Some women are good at this task as well, but we are only going to address the men. I have found that men will hide their depression behind an expression of anger. Anger is such a common emotion for men that they don't mind showing it to everyone.

I have worked with men who cannot keep a job because they have arguments or fights with bosses, other employees, and even customers. These men will always blame someone else for the job loss, never themselves. In fact, depressed men often feel the world owes them something, and that they have a right to be angry with everyone else because of the thoughts and emotions surrounding some issue they haven't resolved from the past. This theory applies to all men with mental issues.

Ladies, beware of how he acts at home on any given day. Does he go from being very happy to very sad in the same day? Is he nice to you, then become very mean at the drop of a hat? Does he continually sleep all day and keep you up all night? Does he lie continually? Is he sneaky? Ask yourself these questions, and then honestly answer them about THAT MAN. If you are not familiar with some of the warning signs of mental illness, look them up on the internet.

Children

A very important aspect of the Secondary Attraction Characteristics is whether or not he wants or has children. A lot of you were devastated when you found out THAT MAN didn't want children. Why were devastated, you ask? When you have put your time and heart into THAT MAN and you find out that he doesn't have the same dreams and vision for the relationship, it destroys you. But the real problem is that you didn't ask him the right questions early on.

When you date a man, it is crucial that you're on the same page when it comes to kids. If you love children, he should too. Watch to see how he interacts with kids — his own, other people's and yours. How does he talk to them? Does he play with them? Is he really interested in their success?

Too many women are getting involved with men who really do not care about children. This is one of the reasons murder and abuse rates of small children are increasing. These men are shaking, choking, and burning these children to death because they were never there for them in the first place. They really only wanted you.

Ladies, you must be the biggest advocates and protectors of your children. Find out if THAT MAN has a criminal record, and before leaving your child with him find out his thoughts on parenting, discipline, education, teen dating and anything else that applies to the wellbeing of your child. If he has kids, ask him questions about their relationship. Who you allow around your children is vital to their survival, and if he doesn't care for his own why would you think he'd do a better job caring for yours?

Women want a man who is committed to his children first, and then to hers. If you are dating a man who regularly visits his children and pays child support, that is a good start. Also, make sure he is involved in their education and their extracurricular activities. A good father plays an integral role in their development on every level. He should be spending quality time with his kids, talking to them, attending their events and attending parent-teacher conferences, as well as helping them with his children.

I love to see a father who knows his children's schedule, keeps his children during the week and not just on a weekend, and who makes their education, not just sports, a priority. This is a father who is concerned and involved in his children's development. This is the type of gentleman that makes for a good life partner.

Social Life

There are many people who live every day with social anxiety, including a number of men. The women who are involved with them don't realize this, and usually believe the man is mean or introverted. Social anxiety is when someone is so afraid of being around people or big crowds that they experience the symptoms of anxiety and would rather stay at home alone than deal with them. For women who are social butterflies, this is hard to understand, which can lead to arguments about how to spend their time.

On the other hand, you may be dealing with a man who only wants to party and hang out. If he is constantly going out with his friends, you need to ask yourself, "Is he truly committed to me? And if so, why does he spend so much time out in the clubs without me? What else is looking for?"

A man who is balanced in his relationships will make sure he spends more time with his girlfriend or wife than with his friends. Of course, this doesn't mean he can't be doing something wrong, but let's pray. Let's have faith in him. When a man is committed to the relationship he will be willing to give up time with his boys to be with his girl. This man understands that the strongest relationship is with his mate. This man will plan everything out for your birthday parties, and organize dates and times for travel. He will also be willing to go to social events with you and for you. Finally, he will be at ease talking to and socializing with those people in your life who are important to you.

The First Sexual Encounter (The Six-Month Rule)

There are many rules that have been discussed on dating and healthy dating boundaries. I have heard of the one-month rule, three-month rule and four-month rule. I have come up with the six-month rule. This is the rule that I believe is best.

Why? Because generally speaking it is the safest and keeps the woman from getting emotionally connected too soon. We have to get back to being patient in relationships and not rushing into deep kissing, grinding or sexual intercourse. These are the emotional connections that are the beginning of the woman's downfall. Let me explain.

We have already discussed how a woman connects to a man through her senses. Once a man says, does, or touches you a certain way, you are all jumbled up inside. See, what happens is every piece of us gets involved with THAT MAN once you start to let your defenses down and allow your senses to take over. Our body wants to feel good and your emotions and senses are vital to this happening.

First, your brain recalls every single moment you were with THAT MAN. The brain begins to focus on the touch you experienced the first time you are with him. Again, remember touch is the fastest way to connect to a person. Your brain says, "Oh, umm, I remember how strong his arms were, how tight he used to squeeze me," and you hold on to this memory. Touch goes deep inside of us. Touch is so powerful.

Think about the times you were upset with THAT MAN and he came over to you, grabbed you from behind and his touch just melted you. Your brain recalls all of this every time he touches you again and again. The smell of him makes you weak in the knees. When you see him you feel sad. When you think of or eat foods that remind you of him, you feel sick, or nauseous, have diarrhea, et cetera.

All of these are reasons to not connect to a man too soon. A man can experience a woman and not have any emotional connection, or he may only have a little connection. This is not the same for the woman. A woman has to work to disconnect from THAT MAN Remember, we are built to hold on to and carry things. We are the receivers.

This is not just psychological, it is physiological. Every time a man enters us, our bodies release hormones, including oxytocin (also known as the "love hormone"), that bond us to him, mentally and in our soul. We don't disconnect once the physical act is over like they do. This is why a woman should not sleep with every man she dates. You will spend some time, maybe years, trying to release THAT MAN out of your mind and soul.

The six-month rule is important because we need to take time to decide what type of man we are actually dealing with. For those who are waiting until marriage, you have nothing to worry about, but others need to wait six months to make sure this man isn't only out for sex or that the relationship will not move fast and burn out. This timeframe takes into consideration that for the first three months most people are on their best behavior, with the man speaking kind words, opening doors for you, not cursing or being mean to you, not taking your money, et cetera.

In months three to six the person's true self begins to be exposed. Most men, even those who are deceitful, will not be able to hold back his true emotions and bad habits for longer than three to four months. The goal is to not go deep with emotional or physical intimacy until after this time. If you choose to do so you put yourself at risk for heartbreak.

Men do not initially think in terms of a long-term commitment, but women do. Sometimes we think, "If I give him some he will commit to me. Women have been fooled for centuries listening to men say, "I can't marry someone I haven't slept with." Or, my favorite: "We have to see if we are sexually compatible before I would ever consider engagement or marriage." If we do not hold ourselves to a higher standard and raise our own self-worth, how can we ever expect the man to do so?

The six-month rule works because you are allowing your intelligence, not your body, to rule your actions. When you are led by your intelligence you do not make decisions based only on your emotions. You do begin to think through your actions, including the consequences of premature sexual activity, including, but are not limited to, guilt, shame, embarrassment, unwanted children, sexually transmitted diseases and being given names by men that women are not fit to be called. So begin to be led by your intelligence, not your body and the feelings that come along with it. We all have heard, "A mind is a terrible thing to waste." A body is a terrible thing to waste too. So use your mind to make well-informed decisions you will not regret later.

Brain

Let's move on to what happens in our brain with regard to relationships. When we enter into a relationship, our brain releases chemicals that cause us to continually think about that person and want to keep connected to them.

Let's start with oxytocin, which as mentioned previously is known as the "love hormone." This hormone can cause a woman to have an orgasm, experience anxiety, activate her maternal instincts, and feel a rush of emotions.

Once you connect with a man emotionally or physically, expect this hormone to play a part in how you respond to him on a daily basis. This hormone is released every time you touch THAT MAN and begin to bond to him. Over time, your bond to THAT MAN becomes very strong.

This is another reason why it is difficult for women to just "move on" to the next man after a relationship ends. You are bonding to THAT MAN every time that hormone is released. For example, when you touch him, your maternal instincts tell you that you have to be patient, kind and loving toward him because that is what a mother would do. Take a break here and do some research on all of the drugs that I am discussing in this section. It is important for us to be educated on how our bodies respond.

Endorphins are the next hormone I would like to discuss. These chemicals help one to "feel good," like after a workout. They also help to release sex hormones. When you meet a man and become excited about the relationship and where it is headed, you release endorphins because you are excited. Again, having sex releases endorphins. Therefore, every time you are intimate with a man, more attachment to him takes place and you feel good and are looking for your next high from no one other than THAT MAN.

When the relationship ends we experience a whole other set of emotions, as well as "withdrawal" from those hormones. This can lead to depression and the many symptoms it causes.

Let's start with the most common symptom associated with depression and that every woman shows outwardly at some point: tearfulness. Crying is one of the ways women begin their healing process when a relationship ends. It may start immediately or a few weeks later, but it almost always happens. So cry over THAT MAN as much as you need to. You will feel better as time goes on and the tears do dry up eventually.

Depression has a wide range of other emotions and physical responses, including hopelessness, low self-esteem, anger, fear, hurt, lack of trust, headaches, stomachaches, insomnia, poor concentration and difficulty with relationships. A few of these are self-explanatory when it comes to breakups, but some need further discussion.

Hopelessness is the feeling that nothing will ever get better. When a woman experiences a breakup her brain says, "You'll never find a man again," or, "Just give up, it's not worth it." Then the woman begins to believe what her brain says and the hopelessness sets in.

Low self-esteem starts next. You will believe you did something wrong or think, "What is wrong with me? Was I not pretty enough? Smart enough? Young enough?"

You always seem to think the breakup is something to do with you being inadequate, and that is not the case. This is a normal grieving process you have to go through to overcome the pain you have experienced.

Anger is another emotion that descends upon you when a relationship ends. This emotion helps you to heal past the hurt you experienced during the relationship. During the healing process everyone becomes angry about the unhealthy behaviors that took place in the relationship. This anger allows you to work through the reasoning in the mind that's telling you moving on is a good thing. Unresolved or unchecked relationship anger, however, is also the reason many men wake up to busted-out car windows, keyed cars, flat tires and even a burned home.

Hurt is another emotion and part of the depression you feel when a relationship ends. This internal pain helps the griever to release all of the mental and emotional pain that has been pent up inside. Some women have described this feeling physiologically, for example: "My stomach is tied up in knots."; "I can't eat or sleep."; "I have diarrhea."; "I'm nauseous." She may even say, "I am having chronic headaches."

Though physiological symptoms of a breakup are very similar to clinical depression, it is actually "situational depression," meaning situations you were in created these emotions and once you work through them you will get better. If one has clinical depression, it doesn't matter what you do. The symptoms will not improve over time without medication and long-term therapy. So take comfort in the fact that this is just temporary.

Relationship Graph

By graphing your past relationships, you should begin to see different and similar qualities in the

men you have dated. Sometimes these qualities are physical in nature.

Many women tend to be attracted to skin color, hair texture, height, weight, facial features, physique, and sense of humor. As mentioned, for some women these primary attraction characteristics can be the beginning of their downfall.

Even though you have been taught to believe, "Beauty is only skin deep," your fixation on appearance — and other primary attraction characteristics discussed earlier — distracts you from what really matters and possibly cause you to miss out on the type of mate you are actually seeking. You also want to map out your secondary attraction characteristics as well.

Graphing your past relationships helps to identify the cycle you've been locked in. These are the patterns, lies, and manipulative techniques by which you continually allow yourself to be misled because of your perception of handsomeness.

Secondly, recognize what needs to be changed in order to get free from this unhealthy relationship cycle. Essentially, it will mean starting a new relationship pattern.

Once you start to recognize your primary and secondary attraction patterns, you will become confident in your ability to not settle for someone who will not meet your needs and be compatible with you for the rest of your life. Once you begin to practice saying no to yourself and that inner voice that tells you, "It's okay to date him because he is nice, cute, et cetera," you will be able to stop dating unhealthy men and start the process of self-cleansing.

The self-cleansing process involves you taking twenty-one days to "fast" from contact with any man. During that time a woman should focus on herself and release all of the negative characteristics and symptoms resulting from her needs on all levels.

After the twenty-one days you should have a better understanding of what you have allowed to happen to you in the relationship. Once you see how you have contributed to your own demise, then it becomes easier to stop the negative relationship cycle.

The women I work with sometimes find it hard to hear and accept that they have contributed to their unhealthy relationship cycle. I understand why this can be difficult. Most women believe, "I did nothing wrong. He cheated on me, stole (or whatever) from me."

While it is true that you didn't commit these acts or deserve what he did, you do need to take responsibility for what you did do "wrong" — that is, continuing to date him and repeatedly forgiving him when you know sooner or later he is going to do it again. You have become addicted to him on some level. Maybe your primary attraction has taken over or you do not want to go through breaking off the relationship. Whatever the reason, when you continue to stay with THAT MAN you are contributing to your own demise.

Of course, no one wants to be alone, but being alone is better than going through continual pain that leads to a lack of trust for men and sometimes women too. This ultimately creates what you didn't want: an unhealthy relationship pattern that causes you to be alone because you cannot trust at all. Do you want to slip into a pattern that perpetually keeps you from meeting the right man?

So go ahead and take a twenty-one-day fast from men and focus on yourself. Then take the next three months to love yourself and identify what you really need. Then you will finally be in a position to get your needs met in your next relationship.

Life will be grand once you create a standard for yourself concerning the type of gentlemen you will date. The man standard you create must be something that is obtainable and not ridiculously out there.

For example, do not say, "I'm going to profile my gentleman after Will Smith or Brad Pitt" or someone else you are not likely to meet on an everyday basis. The model of a man should be created based on your regular circle of friends, places you attend regularly and business circles. I am not saying you can't meet someone out of your normal environment like Brad Pit. I'm just saying be realistic in your creation of your "Male Model Profile."

Commit to this profile on paper, as this will give you something tangible to refer back to and reflect upon. It is important that you understand that this is a framework and no man or woman is perfect; however, creating the profile while be helping in guiding you toward what you are looking for and away from having numerous dates that will go nowhere.

Your profile should consist of six areas of life: Emotional Stability, Financial Stability, Familial Interaction, Mental Health, Physical Health, Sexual Health and Spiritual Health.

Mental: A mentally stable man should be able to communicate to you his thoughts clearly. There isn't a need to try to decipher what he is saying to you on a daily basis. There should not be any mind games in the relationship. He should be honest about his state of mind.

Emotional: A man who is healthy in this regard will have come to grips with where he is emotionally and be okay with expressing any emotion to you, whatever that emotion may be. He will be honest about his needs and concerns.

Spiritual: A whole and healthy person will be able to discuss with intelligence his religious beliefs and views. "I don't have any" is not a good answer! Actually, I recommend staying away from a man who has no God-consciousness. Ninety percent of the time differences in religion end up causing the relationship to terminate.

Financial: Having a mate who is financially stable is very important. Money, or the lack thereof, can mean the difference between a relationship's success or its demise.

A man who comes with a lot of debt will create stress in your life. One of the goals of being in a healthy relationship is to be able to build a life together. That is impossible if both people are not honest about their spending habits, or if they do not create a savings or get-out-of-debt plan.

It is okay to ask to see a person's credit report and inquire about their personal savings plan. This seems to be difficult for a lot of women that I have counseled because they do not want to feel like a "gold digger." My response to this is that you should also share your financial information and growth plan with the gentleman you are dating. Hopefully, this will quiet any suspicions he has of you being a gold digger. Remember, you cannot expect him to have all of his profile pieces in order if yours are not.

Familial: If you're in a healthy relationship, there will be introductions to family members. The immediate families, as well as close friends and close coworkers, should be met within the first six months. If he doesn't introduce you to these key people he probably isn't serious about the relationship.

Also, it is very important to observe how he interacts with his family and friends. Is he disrespectful and angry, or kind, humble, and helpful? These are all signs of who he will be towards you once you get past the honeymoon phase.

Sexual: Sexual history is important in a relationship; however, it is also an area that most of us feel embarrassed about discussing; in fact, some of us would like to avoid it altogether. In these times of HIV and other sexually transmitted diseases, how can someone date a person and not know their sexual history?

I have counseled women who tell me, "I just didn't think it was important" or "I trusted him" and later found out they have contracted some STD or something worse. You are the only person who can make sure that you live to see tomorrow, no one else. Therefore, do whatever it takes to make sure that you live a long life.

One thing you can do is to request his sexual history if you have doubts. You can also go to the clinic together and get an HIV test at the same time. I have worked with couples who have done this early in the relationship and it helped to build trust and security quickly between them.

The goal of the above exercise is to help you create the model profile. Once you have gathered this information, next you have to create a list of questions for your potential mate. Each area is vital to having a healthy relationship. The next step is to formulate several questions surrounding each area, so you become very clear about what your model profile consists of. I recommend that under each category you have at least three questions.

Here are some examples under each area:

Mental: "Have you ever been hospitalized for a mental illness?

Emotional: "How do you manage your anger and stress?"

Spiritual: "How often do you pray in a week, or where do you attend church on Sunday?"

Financial: "If you lost your job today, do you have enough income saved to live on for the next six months?"

Familial: "Why did you and your last girlfriend break up? Tell me about your relationship with your mom."

Sexual: "How many sexual partners have you had? Have you ever contracted an STD?"

Physical: How do you display affection?

These questions are for you to get a good feel for the gentleman you are dating. It is a good idea to try and gather all of this information by date number two. This is an important piece because you can process the information and decide if the man is even worthy of another date. If he doesn't answer at least ninety percent of your questions to your satisfaction, I suggest you ask yourself whether you could be completely and ultimately happy with this man if you married.

Petition

The last section of this book is centered on "Having what you say." If you speak life into the atmosphere, you receive great things. This section is about creating your petition before the Creator.

Ask and you shall receive. You have to speak what you want into existence. We won't open our mouths to speak and therefore we don't receive. We tie God's hands. We constantly try to find the guy and do for him, when the man is supposed to find us and do for us.

When you create your petition for your mate (husband) it has to be very specific. This information is gathered from what you have learned about yourself through self-awareness.

The men you have previously dated in the past and your father all play a part in developing a great petition, as do all of the activities and information you gained from the previous chapters. The petition is to help you realize the ultimate goals set out in this book: to help you learn more about yourself, the reasons you have been involved with the wrong men and ways to learn from those mistakes so it never happens again.

Reading this book is great, but in order for it to be effective you must utilize the techniques that are given. This means implementing them in your life daily and following them always. If you don't follow the rules in their entirety you will not get what you are ultimately looking for in a relationship. I am not saying these steps will get you a husband. What I am saying is following these steps will cut down on some of the unnecessary heartaches women commonly experience, and the situations we often get ourselves into and are too afraid to get out of.

The ultimate goal is to live life well. I hope these steps will be key to helping you live life well and in a healthy relationship.

The petitions consist of combining the information you have learned about yourself and the information you have gathered about old mates you have dated and the new man that is coming to your life.

First, you need to lay out your relationship graph. Second, you will need the information from your Daddy Damage exercise, followed by what you learned about your primary and secondary attraction characteristics. Once you have gathered all this information, look at it again.

Look at patterns in dating, patterns that developed out of your Daddy Damage, and the types of men you were are attracted to in the past. Remember, it's very important to recall your primary attraction characteristics, as these are the behaviors that will continue to keep you stuck in the past and dealing with hurtful issues. In the process, the new you will begin to emerge, creating new relationship behaviors designed to help you have fewer emotional wounds and heartaches in your life.

After you have gathered your personal relationship work and have taken a few days to look it over and process it, you will be ready to create your petition. As you do, it is also helpful to keep in mind what you *don't* want to attract, as this will help you avoid including these things in the petition.

First, start by asking God for His protection and wisdom in all your relationships going forward. Next, ask Him to help you look at all of the unhealthy patterns that you have identified in your past relationships.

Next, ask for His knowledge and understanding of how to be wise in making a decision about what gentlemen to date in the future and even if he is worth dating. Finally, your petition should include the areas of the

Male Model Profile. It should end with you thanking God and some type of closure. Here is an example to help you with this project:

Dear God, thank You for being my father. Thank You for Your hands of protection being upon my life. I also appreciate the wisdom that is given to me daily by Your majestic power. Lord, I come to You today asking for Your help in breaking unhealthy relationship patterns of dating men who are angry, cheaters, manipulative or abusive on all levels and who cannot commit to me.

God, I thank You for giving me the ability to walk away from any man who doesn't have my best interests at heart. Allow me to be secure enough in myself to know that someone is out there for me even when I am alone and feeling lonely. Lord, help me not to settle on a mediocre man just so that I am not alone. Help me to grow in patience and have peace while I am waiting on the man You want to be in my life. Lord, I ask that You send me a man who is mentally and financially sound. Lord, let him have a savings of at least two thousand dollars and let him be mentally and emotionally whole. Lord, allow him to be in good relationship with his family and know how to make and keep strong secure attachments.

Let him be a man who is not afraid to pray, fast, read the Word, and be bold and swift when it comes to his spiritual life and his walk with You. I ask, Father, that you cleanse him sexually and that he doesn't allow his flesh to control his mind or body. Father, let his body be a temple that he doesn't desecrate.

Let him be in good health and be concerned with every aspect of his life. Anything that I have failed to mention, I ask You, God, to fill in the blanks. Let him have goals and let there be no lack in him. Let him have the mind of Christ and let him be healed. Before he enters my life, let every area of his life where he needs to be delivered be completed. In Jesus' name, Amen.

Once the petition is complete, put it in a safe place that is also easily accessible. I recommend that at least once a week you read it out loud to remind yourself of whom you are waiting on and especially when you begin to feel lonely or get tired of being single.

The petition is to be spoken out loud, not read to yourself. Remember, you are speaking things into existence. You are speaking things into the atmosphere and causing there to be movement on your behalf. You are putting into the atmosphere what you want to come forth.

Once this goal is achieved, you are ready to let your new life, with new visions for a healthy relationship, come forth. Now life *will* be grand after THAT MAN, because you no longer accept anyone who doesn't fit the requirements of the petition you created.

Do not settle! Not settling means you may not have a man in your life for some time, but it will be worth the wait. I have worked with some women who followed these steps and within three years they were married to wonderful men. Some of these women dated in that time and some did not. The differences are the quality of men that they encountered. The goal is to remain patient and many good things will happen.

Conclusion

I hope the information I have offered to you in this book has opened your eyes to what has been going on in your romantic life, and that the tools and techniques will be as beneficial to you as they've been to the women I have counseled over the years. Witnessing their pain and healing has been my sacred work, and I thank them for their bravery and willingness to grow, evolve, do something different and new in their dating relationships. Let their stories serve as inspiration to you and know that with patience and self-care, healing — and a healthy, satisfying love — awaits you.